INDONESIA

PAPUA

PAPUA NEW GUINEA

TIMOR-LESTE

TIMOR

TIMOR
SEA

Torres Strait

Cape York

CORAL SEA

INDIAN
OCEAN

Darwin

Arnhem Land

Cape Arnhem

*Cape York
Peninsula*

Cooktown

Cape Léveque

Derby

Broome

*Kimberley
Plateau*

NORTHERN
TERRITORY

Barkly Tableland

*Gulf of
Carpentaria*

(27)

Port Douglas

(24) Cairns

Townsville

Whitsundays

Proserpine

Mackay

GREAT DIVIDING RANGE

Great Barrier Reef

Port Headland

Barrow Island

*North West
Cape*

Great
Sandy Desert

Mount Isa

(23)

(20)

Cape Townsend

Rockhampton

Phosphate Hill   Winton

Great Artesian Basin

Longreach

(22)

Gibson Desert

MACDONNELL RANGES

Alice Springs

QUEENSLAND

Bundaberg

Fraser Island

Carnarvon

WESTERN
AUSTRALIA

Uluru (Ayers Rock)

(27)

*Simpson
Desert*

Birdsville

Caloundra

Brisbane

(21) Gold Coast

MUSGRAVE RANGES

SOUTH
AUSTRALIA

Lake Eyre

NEW SOUTH
WALES

Armidale

Grafton

Geraldton

Great Victoria Desert

Coober Pedy

GREAT DIVIDING RANGE

Coffs Harbour

Bellingen

Kalgoorlie-Boulder

Nullarbor Plain

(4)

(27)

Lake Everard

*Lake
Gairdner*

*Lake
Torrens*

(4)

Broken Hill

Dubbo

(16)

(13) Port Stephens

Perth

Ceduna

Port Augusta

(7)

(4)

Orange

(18)

Newcastle

Freemantle
Mandurah

(3)
(1)
(2)

Bunbury

Great Australian Bight

Adelaide

(6)

Mildura

A.C.T.

(14)
(15)

(19)

Sydney

Wollongong

Nowra

Augusta

Cape Leeuwin

Albany

Port Lincoln

(8)

Gulf of St. Vincent

(5)

Murray

Canberra

(17)

(9)

▲ *Mt. Kosciuszko*

Merimbula

INDIAN
OCEAN

VICTORIA

Ballarat

(12)

(11)

Melbourne

Mount Gambier

Warrnambool

Geelong

Torquay

(10)

Portsea

TASMAN SEA

Bass Strait

SOUTHERN
OCEAN

(26) Devonport

(25) Queenstown

Strahan

TASMANIA

Hobart

PACIFIC
OCEAN

- - - - State boundaries

───── Train lines

⬤ ◯ Cities and prominent towns

0   500   1000 km

0   500 miles

1	The *Australind*	10	*Puffing Billy*	19	Canberra to Sydney
2	Hotham Valley Tourist Railway	11	Melbourne to Ballarat	20	*The Spirit of Queensland*
3	Perth to Fremantle	12	Melbourne to Swan Hill	21	Brisbane to the Gold Coast
4	*The Indian Pacific*	13	Sydney to Brisbane	22	*The Spirit of the Outback*
5	*The Overland*	14	Sydney to the Blue Mountains	23	*The Inlander*
6	Adelaide to Glenelg Tram	15	Sydney to Bowral	24	Kuranda Scenic Railway
7	Pichi Richi Railway	16	Sydney to Armidale	25	The West Coast Wilderness Train
8	Cockle Train	17	Sydney to the South Coast	26	Don River Railway
9	Melbourne to Sydney	18	Sydney to Dubbo	27	*The Ghan*

GREAT RAILWAY JOURNEYS
IN
·AUSTRALIA·
& NEW ZEALAND

GREAT RAILWAY JOURNEYS
IN
·AUSTRALIA·
& NEW ZEALAND

DAVID BOWDEN

JOHN BEAUFOY PUBLISHING

CONTENTS

Opposite: The *TranzAlpine* train on New Zealand's South Island is considered one of the world's great railway journeys.

Pages 2–3: The 'Coffee Pot' train operates on the Pichi Richi Railway in South Australia.

Page 1: *Puffing Billy*'s Baldwin 8A steam locomotive.

INTRODUCTION

In a world where everyone is seemingly trying to get some place as quickly as possible, there is something refreshing and even romantic about the notion of riding a slow train and taking in the journey as much as the destination.

George Stephenson, who drove his train from Liverpool to Manchester on September 13, 1830, probably had no idea just what a momentous step this was in mass transportation. In 1841, Thomas Cook arranged for 500 paying rail passengers to take the train over a grand distance of 12 miles (19 km) from Leicester to Loughborough and so began the era of mass excursions for Britons to see the world.

RAIL JOURNEYS IN AUSTRALIA AND NEW ZEALAND
At the other end of the world, train travel soon developed in Australia and New Zealand too. Railways provided the perfect solution for opening up both countries and for exporting valuable commodities to markets that were mostly in the northern hemisphere.

These days, people in Australia and New Zealand travel freely around their respective countries on planes and in motor vehicles that connect all the main cities and many towns. Others choose to travel on alternative means of transport, such as trains, which still serve an important function in moving people and freight.

Early trains in both Australia and New Zealand involved wagons or carriages pulled by horses along wooden or iron rails. There is some debate about which was Australia's first railway with one suggestion being that it was in 1836 at Port Arthur in Van Diemen's Land (Tasmania) where carriages were hauled by convicts; others claim a rail decline from an 1831 mine in Newcastle as the first. By 1854 a steam locomotive, and the first built in Australia, operated between Melbourne and Hobsons Bay in Victoria.

Before the Commonwealth of Australia became a reality in 1901, Australia comprised independent colonies that adopted different gauges and created problems when standardization between connecting rail systems became necessary.

BIG AND SMALL
Rail is an essential part of the history and present-day life of both Australia and New Zealand. There are differences of course with size the most obvious: Australia is one of the largest rail nations in the world and New Zealand one of the smallest.

At 7.69 million sq km (2.97 million sq miles) Australia is a big country and the world's largest island covering a distance of 4,030 km (2,500 miles) east to west and 3,685 km (2,290 miles) north to south from Darwin to the southern tip of the island of Tasmania. Railways helped open up the continent and develop the economies of the various colonial states that existed before federation.

Most recently the Australian Federal Government, under the Australian Rail Track Corporation, has agreed to build a new $A10 billion freight rail link between Brisbane in Queensland through to Melbourne in Victoria. Known as the Inland Rail Line, it will connect sections of old railway lines into one continuous line of 1,700 km (1,056 miles) and is expected to be completed in 2024. It is lauded as the greatest railway project in Australia of the 21st century. This railway line will speed up the transportation of crops and goods from inland producers to ports for export.

New Zealand, with an area of 269,000 sq km (103,861 sq miles), is one of the world's smallest countries. Its proximity to Australia means that many travellers, especially from the northern hemisphere, holiday to both in one trip. Sea travel linking coastal settlements has always been important for those living in the island nation of New Zealand. While picturesque, its mountainous geography dissected by wide glacial rivers presented engineering challenges in the establishment of its rail network. Long-distance trains have operated in the country for over a century and the golden decades of rail travel were the 1950s and 1960s. There was over 5,689 km (3,535 miles) of rail reach at that stage.

New Zealand has many active railway and heritage preservation groups that work hard to maintain the thrill and excitement of heritage rail journeys. Some of the great railway journeys of the world can be experienced in New Zealand including the *Northern Explorer*, the *TranzAlpine* and the Taieri Gorge Railway.

Australian railway history is important to many enthusiasts and it, too, has various societies championing all things to do with railways. Various state and territory chapters of the Australian Railway Historical Society, for example, produce publications, conduct talks, operate museums and lead rail tours.

In addition to the existing rail network, there are many heritage

and commercial railways in Australia ranging from small operations such as former timber railways to *The Indian Pacific*, one of the world's great trains. Many rail enthusiasts would agree that a list of Australia's other legendary and most popular railways would include *The Ghan*, *The Savannahlander*, *The Spirit of Queensland*, *Puffing Billy*, the Kuranda Scenic Railway, West Coast Wilderness Railway and *The Spirit of the Outback*.

OVERCOMING THE ODDS
Ironically the tracks in both countries have been affected by inclement weather and natural disasters. Bushfires and floods have often wreaked havoc in the Australian bush, while such disasters plus earthquakes, avalanches and landslides have disrupted New Zealand railways. The world-renowned *Coastal Pacific* train between Picton and Christchurch on the South Island stopped operating after the disastrous 2016 earthquake destroyed sections of the line between Blenheim and Kaikoura. For this reason, the train is not documented here.

The Zig Zag Railway in New South Wales was seriously affected by a bushfire and is not yet fully operational. High temperature is another factor that affects the scheduling of some Australian trains, especially during the scorching summer temperatures in Central Australia. Some trains are cancelled during periods of total fire ban or have to operate at reduced speeds. Trains such as *Puffing Billy* in Victoria are always followed by a fire car to check for potential fires generated by sparks.

THE JOURNEY
The beauty, of course, with train journeys is that the scenery is never the same and can be appreciated without distraction. For many dedicated train travellers, it's not so much the destination that's important, but rather the journey itself and the people they meet along the way.

Above: The Puffing Billy Railway Trestle Bridge crosses Monbulk Creek and the Belgrave to Gembrook Road near the train's departure point in Belgrave east of Melbourne.

WESTERN AUSTRALIA

INTRODUCTION

Australia's largest state at 2.53 million sq km (976,790 sq miles) is the second biggest county subdivision in the world (Sakha Republic in Russia is the largest) and covers the western third of the Australian continent. Its capital, Perth, lies just inland on a wide expanse of the Swan River, which flows into the Indian Ocean at Fremantle. The Swan River settlement was established in 1829 by Captain James Stirling. Convicts first arrived in the colony directly from England in 1850 and this continued until 1868.

A privately-managed timber rail line was opened to the south of Perth in 1871. Western Australia's first government railway line ran from Geralton (424 km / 263 miles north of Perth) to Ajana via Northampton. Minerals were transported to the port and a 1,067 mm (3 foot 6 inch) gauge was used here and in other parts of the state.

When the separate Australian states contemplated federating into the Commonwealth of Australia, one of the inducements to get Western Australians to join was the promise of a federally funded rail link from the east to the west. The construction of the standard gauge line from Port Augusta (SA) to Kalgoorlie (WA) was authorized in 1907 and completed ten years later with a break of gauge in the Western Australia mining town. However, it wasn't until 1968 that the standard gauge line between Kalgoorlie and Perth opened. Some gauges in the state converted to standard gauge, others remained narrow gauge and some became dual gauge. Varying gauge widths is something that is very obvious in the state. A suburban narrow gauge commuter service travels between Perth and Midland. To the east and beyond Midland this narrow gauge railway is largely used to transport freight to and from Northam. Meanwhile, a standard gauge link is used to join up with railway lines that head to the eastern states of Australia.

OPERATIONAL INFRASTRUCTURE

Transperth is responsible for managing and operating the Perth suburban public transport network. Transwa operates country trains such as those from Perth to Bunbury and Kalgoorlie.

Western Australia is a major exporter of minerals, gas and oil with some of the largest mines in the world located in remote parts of the state. The private lines of Fortescue Railway, Goldsworthy Railway, Hammersley and Robe River Railway, and Mount Newman Railway are part of the mining industry's essential infrastructure. Freight rail has also been privatized in the state with several companies owning various sections of the track. Another private company, known as Great Southern Rail, operates the famous *Indian Pacific* (see page 18) along the track from Perth eastward through Kalgoorlie in the state and then on to Sydney in New South Wales.

The Western Australia Rail Transport Museum at Bassendean has a representative collection of trains, rolling stock and other railway equipment that was once used in the state. While this collection, belonging to Rail Heritage Western Australia, is mostly from Western Australia Government Railways stock dating back to 1881, it has some locomotives that were also operated for privately owned timber- and gold-mining enterprises. Bassendean was also where Comeng (Commonwealth Engineering) had a

plant, and where various locomotives and diesel railcars, such as those used on the *Australind* (see page 10) were built. Bassendean is located north-east of Perth along the picturesque Swan River and is accessible from Ashfield Railway Station on the Midland Line. The museum is staffed by volunteers and opens on Wednesday and Sunday afternoons.

The Pemberton Tramway Company in the state's south-west operates a short return service from the timber town of Pemberton through the majestic eucalypt forests where karri, jarrah and marri trees thrive. It travels to the Warren River Bridge with stops at the Cascades and Warren River Bridge. This small tram departs daily at 10.45 a.m. and 2 p.m. with a duration of 105 minutes for each journey. There is a small collection of steam trains and carriages at the old station behind the town.

Above: Trains to Mandurah and Perth's southern suburbs cross the Swan River just below Kings Park.

Opposite: Perth Railway Station is the city's major interchange for suburban trains and the terminus for the *Australind*.

THE *AUSTRALIND*: PERTH TO BUNBURY

THE TRAIN THAT THINKS IT'S A PLANE

When it was launched in November 1947, the *Australind*, which operates between Perth and Bunbury, travelled at 63 km/h (39 mph) making it Australia's fastest narrow gauge railway at the time. The three-car diesel hydraulic train (with a capability of accommodating five cars) now travels at a top speed of 110 km/h (68 mph) on its twice-daily services from Bunbury to Perth and back. When the current *Australind* was introduced it was labelled, 'the train that thinks it's a plane' due to its high speeds. It's now the only remaining regional passenger service operating on Western Australia's narrow gauge track.

Australind adjoins the city of Bunbury that was home to the Wardandi people before European settlement. The Dutch were the first European explorers here in 1658 and around 1840, an English-styled village was designed for the area but poor soil and erratic rainfall ended all hopes of sustainable agriculture. Lying 12 km (7½ miles) north-east of Bunbury, Australind is now a satellite township of the larger city and has a population of 12,000.

STATION AND ONBOARD FACILITIES

Onboard facilities include air-conditioning and a complimentary iced-water dispenser. Each car accommodates 40 passengers with seats allocated at the time of booking. Senior citizens travelling from Perth can also enjoy comfortable facilities in a dedicated station lounge.

Refreshments are served from a buffet located in ADP railcars (see below) and include beer and wine but consumption of personal alcohol is not allowed. Toasted cheese and ham sandwiches are 'famous' and these are complemented by a tempting selection of snacks. Newspapers and magazines are also sold but the service ceases 30 minutes before the train arrives at its final destination.

TRAIN DETAILS

The original *Australind* was hauled by U class steam locomotives but in February 1958 these were replaced by X class diesel locomotives. In December 1987, the current ADP/ADQ railcars were introduced and the travelling time was reduced. These railcars replaced the diesel-hauled service (with its vacuum brake train configuration of four coaches with a buffet car and guard van at the rear).

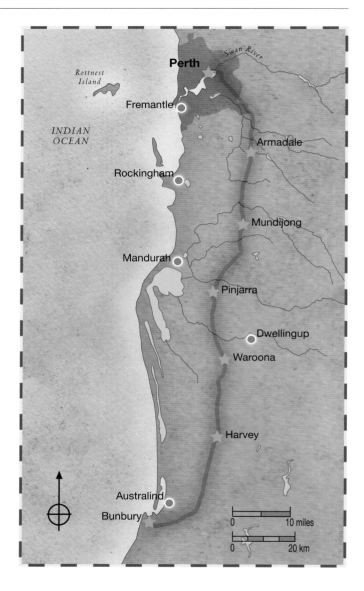

The train is powered by a Cummins KTA19 engine coupled with a Veith transmission. Being diesel hydraulic, the railcars are powered by diesel traction engines coupled to hydraulic transmissions to enable its maximum speed. Railcars with a driver's cabin are classified as ADP railcars and those without a driver's cabin are ADQ railcars. These railcars were constructed at Comeng Bassendean. Transwa has three ADP railcars (numbers 101, 102 and 103) and two ADQ railcars (numbers 121 and 122). The usual three-car configuration has ADP cars at either end with an ADQ railcar in the middle.

Above: The *Australind* stops at several stations including Pinjarra, which is a junction for the line to Dwellingup where the Hotham Valley Tourist Railway operates.

Left: The original Bunbury Railway Station is now the Bunbury Visitor Centre.

When the train was brand new it had a hydrodynamic brake, which used the full horsepower of the main engine to slow the train at speeds above 35 km/h (22 mph) before the friction brakes blended in for a smooth stop. The hydrodynamic brake has been disconnected and friction brakes (disc rotors and pads) are now used.

THE JOURNEY

The *Australind* pulls into Bunbury Passenger Terminal thirty minutes before its scheduled morning departure of 6 a.m. Commuter parking is available in an adjoining carpark and is popular with those travelling to and from Perth in one day.

Named after Australia and India (there was once a belief that land here would be suitable for breeding horses for the British India Army), the *Australind* is a train that caters to Bunbury residents who want to visit the state capital, as well as commuters who work in Perth. Perth students boarding at the Harvey Agricultural College are commonly seen on the train at the end and beginning of their school week. Bunbury is also a coastal resort town that's especially popular with Perth residents travelling here for a day's outing or an extended holiday. The Geographe wine region and the wineries of the Fergusson Valley are just 15 minutes away, while the wineries of Margaret River are 90 minutes to the south. Visitors can travel to the region to swim with or to join a cruise from the Dolphin Discovery Centre to observe wild dolphins, while whale-watching tours depart from Busselton (40 minutes to the south). Closer to town, Koombana Bay in Bunbury is developing into a trendy precinct with bars, restaurants and accommodation.

Bunbury is an important port for the export of grains and minerals; the *Australind* shares the tracks with extra-long freight trains heading to the Bunbury port (mostly carrying alumina from the Alcoa mine at Majurup). While there is talk of a direct and fast train between Perth and Bunbury, no immediate plans are available.

Within minutes of departing Bunbury the train heads east to Picton Junction and past the Picton Aurizon Rail Yard where the train is housed when not operating. It passes housing estates, a light industrial estate and swamplands adjoining the Sanctuary

Golf Resort. From the panoramic windows, the landscape is mostly agricultural with many fields lined with hay bales. Despite its name, the train doesn't go near Australind and passengers from this area normally join the train at Brunswick Junction. Up until the early 1970s, Brunswick Junction was a busy shunting yard as coal trains from Collie and goods trains from Bunbury stopped here.

Along the way, the train stops at Harvey, famous for Harvey Fresh juice, milk and dairy products, and Harvey Beef, rated domestically and internationally as a premium product.

While not immediately obvious, a closer look at the township of Yarloop reveals many buildings, which were destroyed by a bushfire in 2015. Despite concrete sleepers along the track, the train was shut down for a week due to the intensity of the fire and the consequent damage.

Pinjarra has many old locomotives and rolling stock, some of which belong to the Hotham Valley Railway (see page 14). This is the closest railway station to Dwellingup and Hotham Valley, although there is no public transport over the 25 km (15½ miles) between the two destinations. However, there are public buses between Pinjarra and the coastal resort town of Mandurah (30 minute's travel), which is serviced by regular trains of the Transperth system.

OPERATION DETAILS

The *Australind* is operated by Transwa. Train 103 departs Perth daily at 9.30 a.m. (arriving Bunbury at 11.55 a.m.) while train 105 departs at 5.55 p.m. (arriving 8.25 p.m.). In the reverse direction, train 102 departs Bunbury at 6.00 a.m. (arriving Perth at 8.30 a.m.) and train 108 departs 2.45 p.m. (arriving 5.15 p.m.). There are 11 stations along the way but apart from Armadale Station, the train only stops at, from north to south: Byford, Mundijong, Serpentine, North Dandalup, Pinjarra, Waroona, Yarloop, Cookernup, Harvey and Brunswick Junction through advanced bookings.

The *Australind* starts or ends its journey at the Bunbury Passenger Terminal, which is a new station but buses connect to the former Bunbury Train Station and Bunbury Visitor Centre that are closer to the city centre.

Above: The *Australind* in the early morning sunlight at Bunbury Passenger Terminal.

Opposite: The *Australind* operates as Western Australia's last remaining narrow gauge (1,067 mm, 3 foot 6 inch) regional passenger service.

HOTHAM VALLEY TOURIST RAILWAY

RIDE THE OLD TIMBER RAILWAY

The Hotham Valley Steam Ranger train is Western Australia's last remaining steam railway. Taking a trip on it through the eucalypt forests (dominated by jarrah, blackbutt and red gums with banksias, cycads and grass trees in the understorey) is a fantastic family activity.

Western Australia Government Railways (WAGR) developed a network of 1,067 mm (3 foot 6 inch) railway lines north, south and east of the capital Perth. In 1883 a line was opened from East Perth southwards to Pinjarra. By 1910, a branch line up the Hotham Valley extended from Pinjarra to Dwellingup in the Darling Ranges and in later years this continued onwards to Dwarrda.

The Dwellingup timber mill, 97 km (60 miles) south of Perth became the focus for timber sourced from surrounding forests. Timber was transported to Holyoake Mill via several narrow gauge railways until the industry declined in the mid 1950s. A devastating bushfire in 1961 destroyed much of Dwellingup and brought the forestry industry to a virtual end. Limited freight of mostly fruit continued to be carried on the branch line until the mid 1980s but then most activity ceased.

In 1971, a locally based train preservation group became actively involved in establishing the Hotham Valley Tourist Railway (HVTR). They have worked with the WAGR to acquire steam and diesel locomotives, rolling stock and tracks. They continue to work hard to maintain the line and several tourist trains, which now operate from Dwellingup Station. It is the Steam Ranger operating during the cooler months from May to October that attracts much of the attention. At other times, the Dwellingup Forest Train (diesel-hauled) takes over because of the bushfire hazard presented by the steam locomotive.

TRAIN DETAILS

G class steam locomotives once operated on the line with G123 being refurbished. This class became an Australian standard used in most states. They were mostly built by James Martin & Co. of Gawler, South Australia, while others were supplied by Neilson & Co., Glasgow. W class steam locomotives built by Beyer, Peacock and Co. of Manchester, England, also operate on the line with W945 and W920 currently in service.

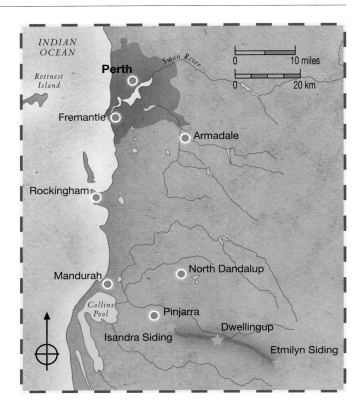

Above: A fully-restored 1919 dining car operates as the Etmilyn Forest Diner on Saturday evenings.

Opposite: Because of the risk of bushfire, diesel-hauled trains operate in the warmer months.

Light diesel mechanical locomotives V4 and V5 operate to Etmilyn Siding on what was once known as the Etmilyn Forest Tramway. These diesel hydraulic trains with Gardiner engines were built by the Drewery Car Co. Ltd in England and started their working life in Tasmania before being purchased by the HVTR.

Various carriages are used; those on the Dwellingup Forest Train are RAP open excursion cars, which began service as RA class. They are medium-sized, open wagons, built in England by the Oldbury Railway Carriage & Wagon Co. as general purpose wagons to carry grain, fertiliser and timber. Imported from South Africa, at least three were converted for tourist excursions and fitted out with aluminium frames and canvas canopies.

THE JOURNEY

Steam Ranger trains head westward for 14 km (9 miles) down from Dwellingup in the Darling Ranges to Isandra Siding about 10 km (6 miles) eastward of Pinjarra located along the main north-south line on which the *Australind* operates (see page 10).

The Dwellingup Forest Train travels eastwards for 8 km (5 miles) from Dwellingup to Etmilyn Siding, twice daily (10.30 a.m. and 2.00 p.m.), every Saturday and Sunday, and on public holidays and selected school holidays from November to April. The return journey takes 90 minutes and the locomotive is repositioned at Etmilyn Siding while passengers enjoy a bushwalk.

The Etmilyn Forest Diner is a restaurant train featuring a fully-restored 1919 dining car where a five-course dinner is served. The train gently negotiates its forest route, which is partly floodlit to add to the ambiance. Trains depart from Dwellingup Station every Saturday and selected Fridays nights at 7.45 p.m. returning at 10.33 p.m. Meals are prepared in the wood-fired oven within the restaurant car that was originally a Commissioner's Carriage.

Private charters for groups and special events are possible.

STATION AND ONBOARD FACILITIES

A shop at Dwellingup Station sells snacks, drinks and souvenirs including a good book selection on local history especially that related to railways; cold drinks are also sold on the train.

Passengers have access to written notes on highlights along the train's route including the vegetation and past land uses. The Forest Heritage Centre in front of Dwellingup Station is worth visiting to learn more about the local history.

Hotham Valley is best known for adventure activities in the forest including mountain biking, forest rope courses, swimming, walking forest trails, canoeing and white-water rafting.

PERTH TO FREMANTLE

CITY TO SURF

Perth lies on the expansive reaches of the Swan River with its port, Fremantle, 19 km (12 miles) to the west. Perth is closer to Asia than to Australia's East Coast and is one of the world's remotest cities, so Fremantle has always been vital for exporting and importing goods. Fremantle, or 'Freo' as the locals know it, is a popular coastal destination both for Perth's 1.85 million residents and for visitors.

European settlers arrived in 1829 to establish the Swan River Colony of Perth. Initially, free settlers came but thousands of convicts arrived later to make a contribution to its development. The Eastern Railway from Fremantle to Perth opened in 1881. Many immigrants, known then as 'New Australians', arrived in Fremantle by boat in the 1950s to start a new life in their adopted land. They brought with them their customs and lifestyles – Fremantle's fishing fleet, Mediterranean food and coffee owe much to this period.

Like many ports, Fremantle was a lively place with sailors keen to release pent-up energy after weeks at sea. However, it became dilapidated and one of Perth's least desirable addresses until a win by an Australian yachting crew in 1983 injected life into the port. For the first time in the race's 132-year history, the Australian team beat the Americans and won the right to host the 1987 America's

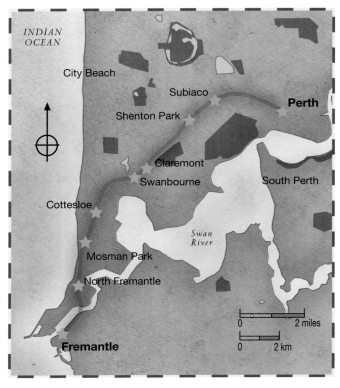

Cup. Fremantle was chosen but it needed a major revitalization to host 29 international yachts and thousands of spectators at the contest off Fremantle. The railway was extended by three stations southward of Fremantle and the Hotham Valley Railway (see page 14) then operated a service on the extended line. Now brimming with vitality Fremantle attracts tourists and locals who especially frequent the 'cappuccino strip' of cafés along South Terrace.

TRAIN DETAILS

The train is managed by Transperth, one of six narrow-gauge lines that they operate. Perth Railway Station has a booking office and ticket machines here and at 70 suburban stations. Fares are calculated by zones and duration for one or a combination of transport modes. DayRider and FamilyRider tickets offer value for multiple journeys while commuters use SmartRider stored value cards.

Modern A-series electric multiple units manufactured by ABB/ADtranz (now Bombardier) and built in Queensland are used. Space is allocated for bikes and wheelchairs, and most stations

Left: Historic buildings within a short walk of the railway station and lining Fremantle's streets are some of the best preserved 19th-century port architecture in the world.

Opposite: While mostly for commuters, this train provides an efficient way of travelling from Perth to the lively tourist precinct of Fremantle.

have bike storage racks. In general, services operate from 5 a.m. to midnight at regular frequencies.

THE JOURNEY

Stops on the 25-minute journey are City West, West Leederville, Subiaco, Daglish, Shenton Park, Karrakatta, Loch Street, Showgrounds, Claremont, Swanbourne, Grant Street, Cottesloe, Mosman Park, Victoria Street and North Fremantle. Announcements and digital signs inform passengers of the next stop.

Trains depart from beneath Perth Railway Station, proceed underground and stop at City West. Once they emerge, the tall buildings of the Perth skyline appear. Many are headquarters for mining companies and an obvious sign of the importance of this industry to Western Australia. While agriculture remains valuable, it's minerals that created an economic boom from the 1950s onwards.

While the route heads north of Kings Park it's within a brisk walk from West Perth and offers commanding views over the Swan River and city skyline.

Express services bi-pass various stations such as from Subiaco to Claremont. Much of the journey passes leafy suburbs and there's some varied vegetation along the way with date palms at West Leederville, gum trees between Subiaco and Daglish, a huge paperbark tree (Melaleuca) at Daglish and grass trees near Swanbourne. Domain Stadium at Subiaco is used for Australian Rules Football matches and concerts. Claremont's stately stone station building is being restored. Claremont Showground is home to the Perth Royal Show held during September or October. Coastal Cottesloe is popular for those wanting to enjoy a day at the beach rated by *Lonely Planet* as the world's second best family beach.

From North Fremantle the train crosses a bridge over the Swan River, a landmark feature of the journey.

The Mediterranean climate makes it ideal for exploring Fremantle on foot with Fremantle Markets, Fremantle Prison, Fine Arts Centre and Maritime Museum being essential sights. Streets are fronted by renovated Victorian buildings now converted to shops, restaurants, bars, cafés and galleries. In the afternoon, it's not unusual for onshore breezes to arrive and cool down Fremantle and Perth. This relieving and refreshing wind is known as the 'Freo Doctor'.

Ferries leave from Fremantle for Rottnest Island and Perth and the recommended journey is to visit Fremantle via train and return via ferry on the Swan River.

THE *INDIAN PACIFIC*: PERTH TO SYDNEY

ONE OF THE WORLD'S EPIC TRAIN JOURNEYS

This is not just one of the great railways of Australia and New Zealand but one of the world's epic journeys stretching across the Australian continent. At 4,352 km (2,704 miles), the *Indian Pacific* route from Perth to Sydney is the second longest in the world after the *Trans-Siberian* and passes through three time zones on its four-day, three-night journey.

TRAIN FACTS

- 30 crew
- 202 passengers
- 28 carriages (guest cars, crew quarters, restaurants, lounges and power cars)
- Two locomotives
- 58,000 litres (15,322 gallons) of diesel fuel per journey
- 3,000 litres (6,340 pints) of water for each carriage
- The train travels 452,608 km (281,238 miles) annually
- 715,000 dishes are served annually
- The kitchen consumes 30,000 litres (63,400 pints) of milk annually
- The bars serve 22,000 bottles of wine annually

Completed in 1917, the train now operated by Great Southern Rail (GSR, which also operates *The Ghan*, see page 116, and *The Overland*, see page 28) is named after the oceans it connects and is a legendary rail odyssey that many travellers aspire to complete.

The actual *Indian Pacific* train only dates back to 1970 when a standard gauge track was completed across Australia. It was the promise of completing the line to Western Australia that persuaded the state to join the Australian Federation in1901. In the 1890s, there was a gap of 1,996 km (1,240 miles) from Kalgoorlie (Western Australia) to Port Augusta (South Australia). However, in 1901 an agreement was struck to bridge the gap and Henry Dean was the engineer appointed to supervise the undertaking. Once the decision to complete the line was made, construction teams worked between 1912 and 1917 to join up the line. One team worked from Kalgoorlie, the other from Port Augusta. They met on October 17, 1917 and, at 10.15 a.m. on October 25, 1917, the Transcontinental Express departed Kalgoorlie for Port Augusta.

Despite the completion, it still required six changes of train from Sydney to Perth to accommodate the various gauges. This was only standardized decades later when on February 23, 1970, an uninterrupted rail link was established from the Indian Ocean

Opposite: Travellers on the *Indian Pacific* from Perth to Sydney quickly discover that Australia is the flattest and driest of all continents.

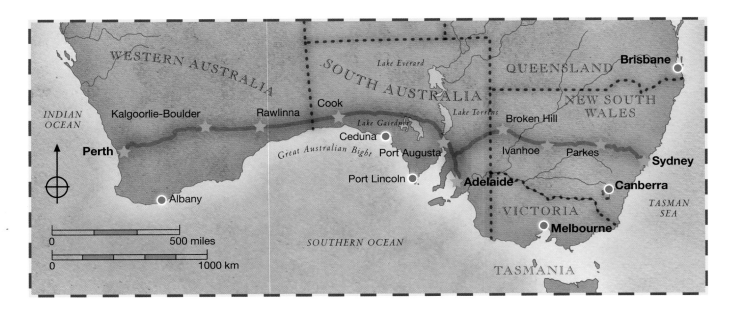

to the Pacific Ocean. This journey took 62 hours and 20 minutes and a crowd of 10,000 met the train in Perth.

TRAVELLING IN STYLE

The glistening 665-m (1,860-ft) stretch of 28 carriages is luxuriously appointed to accommodate 20 Platinum Service beds and 182 Gold Service beds. Platinum Class was introduced in 2016 to offer more space and luxury with a flexible dining format of regionally inspired meals, where dining times are negotiated rather than set as in Gold Service.

It is very much a dream trip for most travellers, almost a rite of passage, particularly for Australian retirees. While the train is normally 28 carriages long this varies based on demand. Packages include all-inclusive dining, beverages and off-train excursions along the way. It is a surreal journey traversing the vastness of Australia in air-conditioned comfort sipping a chilled glass of sparkling wine in the Outback Explorer Lounge or Platinum Club car (the latter having a self-service bar for drinks and snacks).

Restaurant cars such as the Queen Adelaide Restaurant have an adjoining lounge car of comfortable, burgundy-coloured leather seats and a bar. Games and a small library of magazines and books are available, while a musician performs in each lounge car at various times during the journey.

Passengers have choices of single or twin cabin accommodation but the sit-up seats previously designated as Red Service are no longer available. All cabins use the limited space wisely with storage cupboards and drawers, although passengers are urged to carry only their essential luggage on the train and check excess luggage into the baggage car (checked luggage is not accessible during the journey).

Platinum Service passengers enjoy twice as much space as Gold Service with suites (including toilet and shower) being 2.1 m (6.9 ft) wide and 3.6 m (11.8 ft) long. The daytime set-up of a lounge with table, footstools and writing table is converted to either a double or twin bedroom in the evening.

Gold Twin Service is set up as a lounge during the day then converts in the evening to a bedroom when a concealed overhead bed is dropped down by the crew. Gold Single Service (2 m/ 6.6 ft by 1.5 m/4.8 ft) offers the smallest compartments and each carriage holds 18 cabins with shared toilet and shower facilities.

Cabins include safes (the cabin door can't be locked from the outside), tea- and coffee-making facilities and music channels plus an information channel.

Motorail facilities are also available for transporting cars.

Above: Queen Adelaide Restaurant in Gold Service offers passengers two dining service times.

Left: Complimentary beverages enjoyed in the Outback Explorer Lounge are a feature of the *Indian Pacific*.

Opposite page: Some cabins are spacious with a couch (bottom) that staff convert to a bed in the evening.

THE LOCOMOTIVE

The Indian Pacific is hauled by NR class diesel locomotives with a total train weight of 1,103 tonnes (1,216 tons). They are owned by GSR's contract freight company, Pacific National, and were built by Goninan Broadmeadow (Newcastle) or Goninan Bassendean (WA). Each locomotive is powered by a GE Transportation Systems 7FDL-16, 4,000 horsepower engine to enable a fuel-efficient average speed of 85 km/h (53 mph) and a top speed of 115 km/h (71 mph). The carriages were built in the 1960s and 1970s by Commonwealth Engineering in Granville, New South Wales under licence from the Budd Company, Philadelphia.

THE JOURNEY

The train operates two slightly different programmes depending on the direction of travel. The following four-day, three-night itinerary is from Perth to Sydney (west to east) with the reverse journey (Sydney to Perth) being similar but with different timings and some alternative activities. The latter train departs Sydney on Wednesday at 3.03 p.m., arrives in Broken Hill at 6.30 a.m. on Day 2, arrives on the same day in Adelaide at 3.15 p.m. and departs at 9.40 p.m. (with various tour options such as the Barossa Valley vineyards), on Day 3 arrives at Cook at 1.30 p.m. (Central Standard Time) and departs at 1.10 p.m. (Western Standard Time), Rawlinna at 5.55 p.m. and on Day 4 arrives into Perth at 2.57 p.m.

DAY 1

The train departs from East Perth Station at 10 a.m. every Sunday and arrives at Sydney Central Station on the following Wednesday at 11.07 a.m. Passengers gather at East Perth Station for morning tea and music on the platform while the check-in formalities are completed.

Just out of Perth the train passes through Midland and Brigadoon before entering Avon National Park with its picturesque and lush scenery. During lunch, it passes the historic towns of Toodyay and Northam, two of the state's earliest inland towns where agricultural land of wheat, sheep and cattle dominates.

In the early afternoon, there is a change of drivers at Merredin. At dusk the eucalyptus woodlands of Boorabbin National Park show up in stark contrast to the ochre-coloured soils.

Dinner is served as the train forges into the darkness before arriving into Kalgoorlie-Boulder late in the evening and the passengers detrain for an excursion. Settled after gold was discovered in 1893, it is now home to a 3.6-km (2¼-mile) long open mine called the Super Pit. This has operated as a mine around the clock since 1989 and is expected to remain productive until 2029.

DAY 2

With the sun already above the horizon, the train arrives at Rawlinna Station at 6 a.m. and passengers disembark to enjoy breakfast in the open in front of the railway station. Mail is delivered here as well as to the other remote settlements along the route. Established in 1962, Rawlinna is home to 70,000 sheep with the wool sent to Adelaide for classing and exporting. It is a place where jackaroos and jillaroos work Australia's largest sheep station of 1 million ha (2.5 million acres).

Nurina is the next stop where mail is again offloaded before the train embarks across the Nullabor Plain along the longest straight stretch of single track railway in the world at 478 km (297 miles). Interestingly, the vast Nullabor Plains Desert is not an Aboriginal word but rather one with Latin origins meaning 'treeless'. The plains were once a vast sea and the legacy of this is a thick limestone capping that creates an unfriendly environment for tree growth, so there is virtually no tall vegetation across their vastness.

It was unfriendly for Australia's indigenous Aborigines as there were no permanent rivers and very few waterholes. Explorer John Eyre made several journeys of discovery and in February 1841 he

Above: The logo for the *Indian Pacific* is the wedge-tailed eagle, Australia's largest bird of prey.

Opposite: The train makes several stops on its four-day journey and passengers have the opportunity to inspect the diesel locomotives.

Below: An al fresco breakfast at Rawlinna Station served alongside the train is one of the highlights of the Perth to Sydney journey.

successfully crossed the Great Australian Bight from Fowler's Bay just east of the Nullabor Plains in South Australia to Albany in the south-west of Western Australia. In 1870, John Forrest (who became the Premier of Western Australia and acting Australian Prime Minister) retraced Eyre's route from Esperance to Adelaide. In 1873 Ernest Giles failed in his attempt to cross from Central Australia to Western Australia but in 1875 he crossed the nation from Beltana (north of Port Augusta) in South Australia to Western Australia along a route very similar to the one the train follows.

While the train follows an inland route, it runs parallel to the Great Australian Bight and the Southern Ocean as well as the main east-west road known as the Eyre Highway. Just to the north of the railway is the vast expanse of the Great Victoria Desert, Australia's largest desert at 348,750 sq km (134,650 sq miles) and bigger than countries such as Finland, Vietnam and Malaysia.

At Deakin, the train crosses the South Australia border and watches are changed to Central Standard Time (Western Standard Time plus 90 minutes) while passengers enjoy another gourmet

lunch. In the early afternoon the train arrives into the small settlement of Cook and passengers disembark for an hour-long exploratory walk around the ghost town. Before the diesel locomotive era, Cook 'boomed' with 300 residents as it was a water stop for the steam trains using the tracks and there was a school, church, pub, pool and gaol. It effectively closed in 1997 when the line was privatized and officially is now just a refuelling stop with a population of four residents.

Passengers get a sense of the sheer desolation and isolation of the Australian Outback where oppressive temperatures are common. South Australia is the nation's driest state and the railway was important in facilitating the export of the crops grown in the state's 'wheat belt'. Very little survives in the semi-desert with saltbush dominating the landscape and artesian bores providing an essential source of water.

Passengers may see native kangaroos and emus plus feral animals, such as camels (an estimated 100,000 survive in Australia), goats and donkeys although during the heat of the day, most seek what limited shelter there is.

In the course of the evening the train passes Tarcoola where the line divides with the northern line being the domain of *The Ghan* (see page 116) which heads from here through the Great Victoria Desert in Australia's Red Centre and on to Alice Springs and its Darwin terminus.

It passes Port Augusta which is home for the Pichi Richi Railway that operates to the town of Quorn (see page 36).

DAY 3

Just before sunrise, the train has already passed Port Pirie and the junction to Peterborough which the train will return to after a morning visit to Adelaide.

The early sun rises over wheat fields for which the area north of Adelaide is famous. The train inches into the Adelaide Parklands Terminal at 7.20 a.m. and passengers can opt for a bus tour of the city's highlights or a walking tour of the city centre. Those on the guided walking tour explore North Terrace and buildings such as Parliament House, Sir Donald Bradman's statue (the world's most acclaimed cricketer and former resident of Adelaide), South Australian Museum and the Torrens River with views of Adelaide Oval and St Peter's Cathedral.

By mid-morning the train with a completely new crew heads north from Adelaide retracing its tracks to the junction at Crystal Brook and then north-east to Peterborough. In 1880, Peterborough became the centre of several major railway lines and between 1911 and 1914, it was the busiest single track of railway in the world where, on one day, 104 freight and ore trains passed through it. Beside the track is a 1880s Y class steam locomotive and the Steamtown Heritage Rail Centre is situated in the town.

By late afternoon the train arrives into Broken Hill Station 1,207 km (750 miles) west of Sydney. Minerals were discovered in nearby Silverton in 1875 and in Broken Hill in 1893, and it became acknowledged as the world's richest single silver, lead and zinc deposit. The Broken Hill Proprietary Company Limited was formed in 1885 to extract the minerals and this later became BHP, one of the world's biggest mining companies.

Many called Broken Hill 'Silver City' and while situated in the far west of New South Wales it is as much in tune with Adelaide as Sydney and has adopted Central Australian Time. This has its historic roots in the decision to export Broken Hill's ore via rail through South Australia rather than New South Wales. The Silverton Tramway Company was created to build a line from Cockburn in South Australia 50 km (31 miles) to Silverton, which was later extended to Broken Hill. This enabled ore to be transported from the mines to the smelters in Port Pirie in South Australia.

In 1887, the first Y class steam locomotive, operated by South Australian Railways, arrived in Silverton and trains ran on these tracks until 1970. By 1933, the train operator had 20 steam locomotives and 660 goods wagons. The line from Sydney to Broken Hill only opened in 1919.

Broken Hill is also home to two iconic Australian institutions – the Royal Flying Doctor Service and School of the Air. The former provides emergency medical air support to remote communities and the latter an education to children in remote areas via radio communications. Passengers on the *Indian Pacific* can opt to see some of the city sights, a local art gallery or enjoy a show based upon the 1994 movie, *The Adventures of Priscilla, Queen of the Desert*, which was filmed locally. Many films and television advertisements have been filmed here and in Silverton.

After dinner and during the evening and early morning of the next day the train passes Menindee, Ivanhoe, Condobolin, Parkes, Orange and Bathurst.

DAY 4

By daybreak, the train has crossed most of central New South Wales and breakfast is taken as the train crosses the Blue Mountains (see also the journey from Sydney to the Blue Mountains, page 62).

The train passes Bell, Mount Victoria, Medlow Bath and Katoomba with parts of the vast Blue Mountains National Park visible on the southern side of the carriages.

From the Blue Mountains, the train descends some 1,000 m (3,450 ft) to the base of the escarpment, and on to the Cumberland Plain and the western extremities of suburban Sydney. By late morning the train arrives into Sydney's Central Station.

Above: The train makes an extended stop at Broken Hill where passengers can appreciate the importance that mining for silver, lead and zinc has here.

Opposite: Now a ghost town, Cook once was a thriving community with its own gaol.

SOUTH AUSTRALIA

INTRODUCTION

South Australia has a unique rail history in that it is one of the few places in Australia and the world to have all three rail gauges: broad gauge (1,600 mm/5 foot 3 inch), narrow gauge (1,067 mm/3 foot 6 inch) and standard gauge (1,435 mm/4 foot 8½ inch). It was also the only Australian state not to receive convicts and its capital, Adelaide, is a planned city with large expanses of parklands around the centre and along the banks of the Torrens River that flows through it.

In 1834 the British Parliament passed the South Australian Colonisation Act to enable emigration to this part of Australia. The South Australia Company was formed, a colony was proclaimed in 1836 and Adelaide settled as the capital in 1837. The state covers an area of 984, 000 sq km (379,925 sq miles) or 12.8 per cent of the Australian landmass.

In 1854, an iron rail line was built to link the Murray River and wharfs at Port Elliot and Victor Harbor. Like many Australian railways, it was developed to facilitate the export of rural produce from inland farms and cattle stations to global markets. This line is now incorporated into the Cockle Train (see page 38).

The first steam railway in the state opened in 1856 and operated from Adelaide to Port Adelaide using rails of the same type as the Great Western Railway in England. They were known as baulk track of wrought-iron rails laid on longitudinal sleepers at a gauge width of 1,050 mm (5 foot 3 inch). They proved unsuitable and were replaced by 1868. The first three locomotives were made in Manchester and shipped to South Australia in 1856.

Adelaide's flat terrain made it ideal for horse-drawn trams with the first line to Kensington Park being opened in 1876. In 1907 the Municipal Tramways Trust was formed to take over the horse-drawn trams replacing them with electric trams (the last horse tram operated in 1912). The first electric tram began operations in 1909 with many cars (known as 'toastracks') being locally built.

A HISSING HUB

Peterborough (formerly Petersburg) north-east of Adelaide, is a historic railway town that was a leading regional rail maintenance and service town for the state's trains and rolling stock. It is strategic in many ways as is located half-way between Perth and Sydney and 2.5 hours from Adelaide. The town has been described as a 'hissing steaming hub of mighty locomotives at the crossroads of a growing nation'. In its heyday, up to 100 steam trains passed through the town and it is one of only two locations in the southern hemisphere where three gauges track next to each other (Gladstone is the other). While the volume of trains has diminished, Peterborough still witnesses Australia's two iconic trains in *The Ghan* and *Indian Pacific* passing through.

In 1881, the line from Port Pirie arrived in the town via Gladstone and Jamestown and in 1887, the line to Silverton and Broken Hill in neighbouring New South Wales opened. The link to New South Wales was important as it extended the line towards Australia's populated east coast and in 1917 the Transcontinental from Perth to Sydney commenced operations. In 1929, *The Ghan* from Adelaide to Alice Springs first passed through the town.

In the mid 1920s, one third of the town's population of 4,000 worked for the railways but diesel locomotives and the introduction of standard gauge in the 1970s seriously affected employment, and the closure of the railways in 1990s saw a dramatic drop in the population. However, Peterborough's connection to the railway lives on through the efforts of enthusiastic volunteers who run the Steamtown Heritage Rail Centre in the town centre. The Centre is based in former railway workshops. The turntable and roundhouse are the main features of the exhibit with the turntable being unusual in that it accommodates the three rail gauges.

Another repository of railway rolling stock and exhibitions is to be found at the National Railway Museum in Port Adelaide. What is reputed to be Australia's largest railway museum houses over 100 exhibits mostly from South Australia and Commonwealth Railways. It also operates the Semaphore to Fort Granville Tourist Railway.

Opposite: The tram to Glenelg passes through Adelaide's Victoria Square.

THE OVERLAND: ADELAIDE TO MELBOURNE

GRAINS, GRAZING AND GOLD

Every Monday and Friday morning *The Overland* pulls out of Adelaide Parklands Terminal for the 10½-hour journey through to Melbourne's Southern Cross Station on Spencer Street in the Victorian capital. It makes the return journey from Melbourne every Tuesday and Saturday morning and covers a distance of 828 km (515 miles) at an average speed 85 km/h (53 mph).

A service between the two state capitals started in 1887 and was known as the *Intercolonial Express*. Not long after, the name changed and, depending on where you got on the train, it was known as the *Adelaide Express* or the *Melbourne Express*.

It operated as a night train using various sleeper carriages imported from the United States, initially supplied by Mann Boudoir Car Company and then Pullman. By 1990, the train was hauled by two N class diesel locomotives and included a carriage for transporting cars, sleeper carriages, sit-up carriages, a club car, buffet car and a luggage car. By 1995, Australian National operated the service with two CLP class diesel locomotives and the entire track traversed recently standardised broad gauge rails.

Above: The train's logo is an emu.

Opposite: Passengers departing on *The Overland* from the Adelaide Parkland Terminal can also see trains such as *The Ghan* standing on an adjoining platform.

In 1997, Australian National was sold, Great Southern Rail acquired the rolling stock and National Railway was contracted to operate mostly NR class diesel locomotives. Not long after,

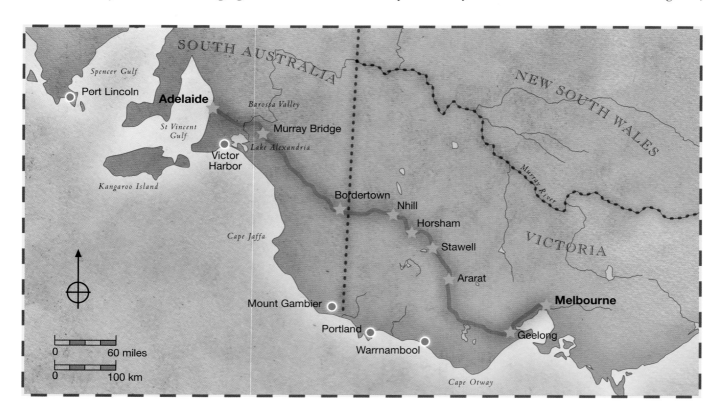

Above: *The Overland* travels at an average speed of 85 km/h (53 mph).

Right: Seating in Red Service is spacious with panoramic windows giving views of the ever-changing landscape.

Opposite: Snacks and beverages are sold in Café 828.

the night train was suspended, day frequencies reduced and some stops were eliminated from the schedule.

The service was refreshed in 2007 with a new livery, interiors and logo but with a reduced schedule of just twice weekly departures.

The Parklands Terminal was originally built as a dual gauge facility accommodating standard gauge trains such as the *Indian Pacific* and *The Ghan* for northbound trains and the broad gauge of *The Overland* heading eastwards. Great Southern Rail also operates *The Ghan* (see page 116) and the *Indian Pacific* (see page 18).

STATIONS AND ONBOARD FACILITIES

The Overland departs from Parklands Terminal (also known as Keswick Terminal after the suburb in which it is located) where the platform is long enough to accommodate *The Ghan* and the *Indian Pacific*, which both use it as well as the six-car, *The Overland*. The terminal opened in 1984 and there is a ticket office although most passengers pre-book their journey. Passengers are checked in at an airport-style counter and up to 40 kg (88 lb) of luggage can be sent through to their destination (checked bags are not accessible during the journey). For unchecked luggage, the above-seat racks

are large enough for most bags and there is an area near each door for larger cases. There is no overnight storage for luggage available at the station.

Red Service and Red Service Premium are offered with the latter being more spacious and providing more personalised services, such as extra seating space, complimentary in-seat, à la carte meals, non-alcoholic drinks served from a trolley, individual reading lights, a welcome drink and an additional 10 kg (22 lb) of luggage allowance.

Red Service accommodates 60 passengers per carriage comprising two seats either side of a central aisle; seating is spacious (45 degree incline and 49 cm / 19 in leg space). A fold-out table is concealed within the armrest. Seating in Red Premium is based on three seats across (doubles and a single either side of the aisle with 36 seats per carriage) and 67 cm (26 in) leg room.

Café 828 is a dedicated car serving snacks, drinks and substantive meals. Some vegetarian dishes are offered as is beer and wine by the bottle. Cream teas have universal appeal and are a speciality item for the afternoon. Souvenirs are also sold at the café counter and there is comfortable seating in the carriage for enjoying a meal

and the passing scenery. A food and drinks trolley also makes regular rounds of the passenger cars. There is no wi-fi onboard and mobile phones may not work on some remote stretches of the track but there are sockets for charging electrical devices.

THE JOURNEY

Within 15 minutes of departing Adelaide the train is already travelling through forested areas as it climbs the Adelaide Hills through suburban stations such as Blackwood, Belair and Mount Lofty. Here gnarly gum trees cast shade over a lush understorey and then a few vineyards dot the landscape near Mount Barker Junction. Olive groves can also be seen to remind passengers that South Australia's climate is mostly Mediterranean. A member of the train crew provides informative commentary of the stops along the way and the countryside through which the train passes.

Within 90 minutes from Adelaide, the landscape is rolling open countryside dominated by fields growing crops such as wheat. Wheat and sheep have been always been important to the Australian economy and many towns along the way have large silos and bunkers by the track for storing harvested grains. Beef and sheep are grazed on the land and a variety of other crops are grown.

The first stop is Murray Bridge just a little over two hours out of Adelaide, bridging the river of the same name. The first bridge was erected in 1879, and used as a joint road and rail bridge; a new, dedicated rail bridge was built in 1925. What was originally called Edward's Crossing was renamed Murray Bridge in 1924 and in 1979 the new Swanport road bridge opened downstream from the town eliminating much of the town's through traffic. Paddle steamers also operate on the river from Murray Bridge with a range of multi-day cruises on offer.

The train makes a picturesque traverse along cliffs above the Murray River to Tailem Bend just north of where the Murray River empties into Lake Alexandria. Once a major railway junction, branch lines radiate from here to transport grains harvested within the Murray Mallee. The countryside is completely flat and after Murray Bridge the train hits its top speed on its journey to Bordertown, the last town in South Australia.

At noon, the train crosses into Victoria at Serviceton, once an important stop for the train. Its train station was completed in 1889 when the railways of Victoria and South Australia met and from 1928 until the mid 1930s, a dining car operated on the train from Adelaide to Serviceton.

While *The Overland* now travels past the old station without stopping, Serviceton had its moment of glory when American singer Tom Waits wrote about it in his 1983 song *Town with No Cheer*. In the song, Waits sings about the demise of the town and about how the local farmers and graziers wouldn't now be able to get a drink on the journey from Melbourne to Adelaide on *The Overland*.

Drinking in the local pub is very much part of Australian bush culture especially in the parched lands of Victoria and South Australia through which the train passes. This is brought home as the train passes near places like Little Desert National Park on its way to Nhill and Dimboola.

At Dimboola around 1 p.m. the crew of the National Pacific diesel locomotive change but passengers getting on and off in these remote parts of western Victoria can be counted on the fingers of one hand.

At Horsham, 300 km (186 miles) west of Melbourne, the distant countryside to the south opens up to the undulating range called the Grampians. Horsham is located on the floodplain of the Wimmera River and the land to the north supports dry land farming.

The next towns of Stawell (pronounced *stawl*) and Ararat were founded on gold discoveries, first found in the former in 1853. In addition to being a gateway to the Grampians National Park, the Stawell Gift, Australia's richest footrace is contested here every Easter on the 120-m (131-yard) long grass track at Central Park.

At 2.45 p.m. the train pulls into Ararat station located opposite the Old National Hotel. Ararat is also the terminus for the Ararat V/Line service from Melbourne. The town was founded by Chinese gold miners in 1857 when the Canton Load was unearthed in one of the frenzied rushes that occurred across Australia. Ararat, like Stawell, was the centre of one of several gold rushes of that time. Victoria alone witnessed its population boom from 76,000 in 1851 to 540,000 by 1861 on the back of these gold rushes. Visitors to the town can learn more about this era at the Gum San Chinese Heritage Centre.

On a hill above the town the grand establishment called Aradale dates back to 1860 and for much of its time was a mental health institution but is now a TAFE College where many students acquire winemaking skills which they put into practice in the district's wineries.

Not long after Ararat the rail line splits with a track heading north but *The Overland* veers to the south on its journey to Geelong and Melbourne. *The Overland* pulls into Geelong (North Shore) at 5.30 p.m. but has to make two stops because the

platform here is not sufficiently long to accommodate the whole train. Then it makes its final run through the mostly industrial suburbs of southern Melbourne into the Southern Cross Facility in downtown Melbourne.

Above: The train from Adelaide terminates in Melbourne.

Opposite: *The Overland* crosses the Murray River at Murray Bridge, South Australia's fifth largest urban area with 18,000 residents.

ADELAIDE TO GLENELG TRAM

A DAY AT THE BEACH

South Australia's population is 1.7 million with its capital Adelaide being where most live (population 1.25 million). The tram from the city to beachside Glenelg is so popular that everyone has fond memories of journeys on it. Glenelg is where the Colony of South Australia was proclaimed in 1836 and has always been a place for recreation. Located along Holdfast Bay on St Vincent Gulf, the sands and gentle surf have ensured its popularity.

Initially horse-drawn coaches ran from Glenelg to Adelaide, then two private steam train services commenced operating; one from Adelaide's King William Street following the route of the present tram and the other from Adelaide Train Station on North Terrace. The former, known as the Adelaide Glenelg and Suburban Railway started in 1873 and the latter, the Holdfast Bay Railway, opened in 1880. These companies merged but in 1899 the government acquired the merged company.

In 1879, a railway was built to Marino 6 km (3¾ miles) south of Glenelg but this was short-lived. However, a horse-drawn tram operated for 30 years before the Adelaide to Brighton Railway was built in 1913.

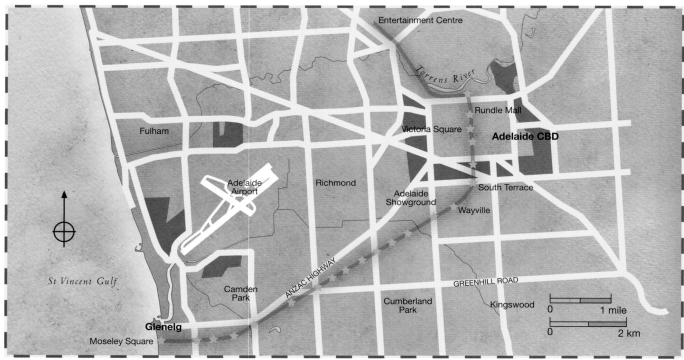

In 1909, Adelaide introduced electric trams and in 1929 the service was extended to Glenelg. Type H tram cars were designed by the Municipal Tramways Trust's Chief Engineer, W.G.T. Goodman and built locally by A. Pengelley & Co.

In 1958, diesel buses replaced all of Adelaide's trams except the Glenelg service. Type H trams remained in service until 2006 and in 2007 the Glenelg route was extended through the city to North Terrace, then to the Entertainment Centre in 2010. There are proposals to extend the network including four loop extensions to Unley, Norwood, Port Adelaide, Prospect and Henley Beach.

TRAIN DETAILS

The distinction between a train and a tram is hotly debated with the main difference being that a tram (trolley, streetcar or light rail) shares its tracks with other vehicles such as a road with cars, whereas a train operates on a dedicated route. The Adelaide to Glenelg Tram does both on its 15-km (9-mile), 28-stop journey (the train only halts at smaller stops upon request).

German Flexity, low-floor trams (single-deck, electric multiple units) made by Bombardier, and French Citadis (Type 302) trams made by Alstom are now in service. Citadis trams were purchased from Madrid, Spain as they were surplus to their requirements. These have a capacity of 186 passengers while Flexity trams accommodate 170. Trams run mostly every ten minutes from 5 a.m. to 11.30 p.m., Monday to Friday, with later starting and finishing times at weekends.

THE JOURNEY

Trams for Glenelg start from the Entertainment Centre in Hindmarsh and continue for another ten stops to South Terrace. This marks the end of the free inner city system, from here onwards to Wayville and stations just short of Glenelg, fares are charged. Fares vary from peak to non-peak times and tickets can be purchased from onboard machines.

From the Entertainment Centre trams head southwards before turning into Adelaide's grid-system central business district, laid out in 1837 by Colonel William Light. The route passes the New Royal Adelaide Hospital on North Terrace, the Adelaide Convention Centre, Adelaide Casino (located in the grand sandstone building of the former Adelaide Train Station; the original was built in 1856 and the present one in 1928) and Parliament House before turning south along King William Street.

The Rundle Mall stop accesses the retail thoroughfare of the same name. Victoria Square is the stop for the Adelaide Central Market. At South Terrace, the tram exits the central business district and heads through parklands, which fringe Adelaide on all four sides. Once out of the centre, the tram passes through mostly leafy suburbs. On race days, trams halt at a dedicated stop for the Morphettville Racecourse.

After 50 minutes, it terminates in Moseley Square at the end of Jetty Road. At the head of the square is the impressive bluestone building that was once Glenelg Town Hall and is now the Bay Discovery Centre. This houses an impressive display of the local area including information on the tram and local buildings.

Above: The Glenelg tram passes several grand buildings such as St Andrew's by the Sea Church on Jetty Road Glenelg.

Opposite: An old 'red rattler' tram is displayed in Wigley Reserve Glenelg.

PICHI RICHI RAILWAY: PORT AUGUSTA TO QUORN

RIDE PART OF THE ORIGINAL GHAN ROUTE

South Australia's Flinders Ranges have one of the state's most unique and dramatic landscapes. The state's largest mountain range, which extends for 430 km (267 miles) from Port Pirie northwards to the mostly dry salt expanse of Lake Callabonna, has a semi-arid climate.

The railway arrived in Quorn, 39 km (24 miles) north-east of Port Augusta and 333 km (207 miles) of Adelaide, in 1879. From here it progressively moved northwards to reach Alice Springs in 1929. For a town of just 1,000 residents, Quorn had an important role to play when the north-south railway (Great Northern Railway and later, Central Australia Railway) was united with the east-west railway (Trans-Australia Railway) in 1917. However, Quorn's importance diminished in 1937 when the standard gauge railway opened between Port Pirie Junction and Port Augusta, and east-west trains subsequently bypassed the town. In the 1950s, a new north-south route resulted in all but a few freight trains operating the route but they too ceased in 1980.

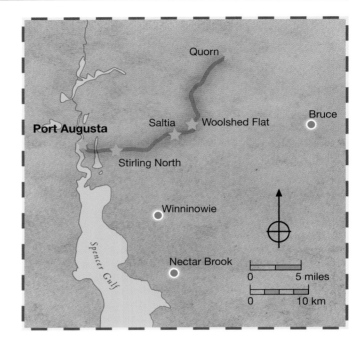

Right: The 'Coffee Pot' train is an Edwardian-era steam railcar and the last operating example of its type in the world.

Opposite: Tourist heritage trains of the Pichi Richi Railway operate during the cooler months from March to November.

Now visitors to the region have the opportunity to ride on part of the original *Ghan* route (see page 116) between Port Augusta and Quorn through the efforts of the hardworking volunteers of the Pichi Richi Railway Preservation Society. It was initially formed in 1973 to preserve the railway infrastructure but this later included the operation of heritage tourist trains. These trains operate between March and November at weekends, on public holidays and on some days of the school holidays. The society makes a valuable contribution to local tourism.

THE TRAIN

Two services are operated: the *Afghan Express* departs from Port Augusta to Quorn and back, and the *Pichi Richi Explorer* from Quorn to Woolshed Flat half-way through the pass and back.

Trains used on this narrow gauge service are either restored historic steam or diesel locomotives with the final choice based on the time of year and the weather. When there is a risk of bushfire, a diesel locomotive may replace the steam. All trains move at a relaxed pace and passengers get to ride in immaculately restored carriages that are up to 100 years old.

The steam locomotive NM25 hauls the *Afghan Express*. The class of 4-8-0 locomotives was introduced in 1925 on the Central Australia Railway service between Port Augusta and Alice Springs. Its design was based on Queensland Railway's C17 class but by 1954, diesel locomotives were operating on the route with the last journey by NM25 being in 1964. In their day, NM class locomotives hauled *The Ghan* and other services along the route.

Two diesel locomotives support the steam locomotive. NSU52 is a Sulzer-powered design built in England at the Birmingham Carriage and Wagon Company. It was one of 14 of this class that entered service in 1954 with NSU52 being the first to pass through the Pichi Richi Pass and on to Quorn. The other, NT76 ('N' meaning narrow and 'T' Tulloch) is one of 13 of the class built to back up the NSUs but built in Australia by Tulloch Limited of Rhodes, New South Wales. Only NT76 remains.

A unique service that operates out of Quorn is the 'Coffee Pot' train, an Edwardian-era steam railcar. This engine was built by Kitson and Co of Leeds, England in 1905 and this is the only one of its type operating in the world. Occasional services with just 22 passengers depart from Quorn at 12 noon and return by 4.30 pm.

THE JOURNEY

Passengers on full (*Afghan Express*) and half-day (*Pichi Richi Explorer*) excursions can admire the scenery of an ancient landscape along the route.

The *Pichi Richi Explorer* departs Quorn at 10.30 a.m. and returns at 1.00 p.m. covering a return distance to Woolshed Flat of 32 km (20 miles). It passes through a semi-arid landscape and through deep rock cuttings of ancient geological formations. Passengers can get off the train at Woolshed Flat where light refreshments are available.

Afghan Express trains depart from Port Augusta at 10.30 a.m. and return by 4.30 p.m. with a two-hour stop in Quorn where passengers can explore the historic town. Soon after leaving Port Augusta the train travels across the red earth plain that is punctuated by low, scrubby, bluebush vegetation. The return journey covers 78 km (48 miles). Roughly a third of the way into the journey, the train starts to climb up through the Pichi Richi Pass and the Flinders Ranges.

THE COCKLE TRAIN: GOOLWA TO VICTOR HARBOR

A DAY BY THE BEACH

This train is named after the cockles that early passengers sought at the beaches along the coastal route that the track traverses (and an earlier horse-drawn train) from Goolwa to Port Elliot and Victor Harbor on South Australia's Fleurieu Peninsula.

Famed for its rolling hills, farmlands, national parks, coastline and vineyards, the peninsula was named after a French explorer by fellow Frenchman Nicolas Baudin. In April 1802, Baudin met English navigator Matthew Flinders offshore from the Cockle Train's current route giving the name to Encounter Bay.

In the late 18th century, American whalers hunted Southern Right Whales offshore and today, Middleton ('Middle Town'), a small station along the route, is especially popular for whale watching from May to October.

Goolwa is one hour south of Adelaide (89 km/55 miles) and located near the mouth of the Murray River. The combined Murray-Darling Rivers extend for 3,750 km (2,330 miles) and flow into the Great Australian Bight and Southern Ocean near Goolwa.

TRAIN DETAILS

What is Australia's oldest steel-railed railway dating back to 1887 was built to link the Murray River and wharfs at Port Elliot and Victor Harbor. It and SteamRanger trains are operated by volunteers of the Australian Railway Historical Society (SA Division).

400 class 'Redhen' railcars are mostly used, although on some services, locally restored 'Brill' railcars operate while steam locomotives 621 and Rx207 are used on this and other SteamRanger services. The railcars are fully restored with spacious seating and have wheelchair access.

THE JOURNEY

Year-round, Wednesday and Sunday departures leave from Goolwa where the train is based and proceed 21 km (13 miles) on the 30-minute journey to Victor Harbor.

Trains depart from the Goolwa Wharf, which was once a thriving river port and the only place in Australia where paddle steamers and steam trains met to transport produce. One-hour

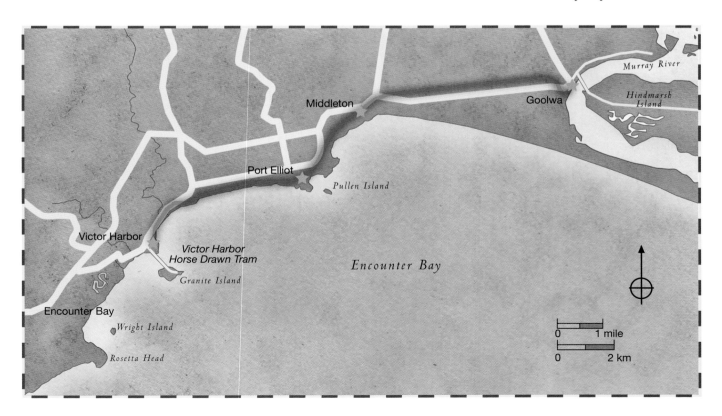

weekend cruises on the historic paddle steamer *PS Oscar W*, built in 1908, depart from Goolwa. Passengers should time their visit to coincide with markets at Goolwa Wharf on the first and third Sundays of the month and Victor Harbor on the second and fourth Sundays.

The train traverses the farmland plains beyond Goolwa towards Middleton where the train stops on request.

Picturesque Port Elliot features the sweeping Horseshoe Bay beachfront protected by offshore islands. Whale watching from the cliffs is popular while exploring the town's historic bluestone buildings is recommended as is the railway museum at the station.

From here, the train follows the scenic coastline where houses have commanding views of the turquoise waters of the bay. Just after Port Elliot the train crosses the Watson Gap viaduct, passes Chiton Surf Life Saving Club, crosses Hindmarsh River and goes past sporting facilities on the outskirts of Victor Harbor. While several road crossings en route are operated automatically, the final crossing into Victor Harbor is opened and closed manually.

The train arrives in Victor Harbor Station on Railway Terrace lined with majestic Norfolk Island pines. Nearby, an historic horse-drawn tram heads along a causeway to Granite Island. Victor Harbor is a busy seaside town with many attractions including a Penguin Rehabilitation Centre plus the Encounter Coast Discovery Centre featuring Aboriginal, whaling and

railway history. The train is turned around in Victor Harbor on a 30-m (98-ft) electric turntable.

Trains depart Goolwa at 10 a.m., 12.15 p.m. and 2.45p.m. and Victor Harbor at 11 a.m., 1.30 p.m., and 3.45 p.m. with additional services during peak seasons.

In the event of high temperatures and total fire bans, diesel locomotives are substituted for steam engines but the Cockle Train doesn't operate when temperatures exceed 35°C (95°F).

STEAMRANGER

SteamRanger also operates several heritage steam- and diesel-hauled tourist trains including a service between Mount Barker, Strathalbyn, Goolwa and Victor Harbor. Mount Barker is located in the Adelaide Hills 33 km (21 miles) south-east of Adelaide.

The Southern Encounter Steam Train operates during school holidays and the first and third Sundays of the month from June until the end of November. It travels through the southern Mount Lofty Ranges to Strathalbyn, across the Currency Creek viaduct and into Goolwa before heading to Victor Harbor where there is a three-hour stop before it returns. Trains depart at 10 a.m. returning to Mount Barker at 6.05 p.m. Infrequent services also operate between Goolwa and Finniss.

Above: The train travels along the beachfront between Victor Harbor and Goolwa.

VICTORIA

INTRODUCTION

The former Port Phillip District became the Colony of Victoria in 1851. Victoria covers an area of 227,600 sq km (87,877 sq miles) or three per cent of the total country. Its capital Melbourne has a comprehensive electric railway network operated by Metro Trains Melbourne for the Victorian Government. The suburban lines were electrified as early as the 1920s. It now operates 207 stations on 16 lines plus a city loop covering over 300 km (186 miles) of electrified track and facilitates more than 230 million passenger journeys per annum.

The term 'meet me under the clocks' is part of the local vernacular and refers to the train destination clocks at Flinders Street Station where many people in Melbourne meet before heading off into the city.

THROUGH THE AGES

The Melbourne and Hobsons Bay Railway is credited as Australia's first common-carrier steam railway, which began transporting passengers in September 1854. The train, built by Roberston, Martin Smith and Co., was also the first constructed in the southern hemisphere and had a maximum speed of 40 km/h (25 mph). The 4-km (2½-mile) long track ran from what today is Flinders Street Railway Station to Sandridge (now Port Melbourne).

Soon after, the Melbourne to Geelong line opened in 1857 to become the state's first country railway. In 1883, the state became connected by rail to New South Wales when the line from Melbourne to Wodonga joined the Sydney to Albury line at the New South Wales-Victoria border. However, the trains were of different

gauge necessitating a change of trains for passengers. In 1887, the rail connection between Melbourne and Adelaide was opened.

From 1884 onwards, train travel increased throughout Victoria after the colonial government agreed to open almost 60 new lines. Steam trains operated the lines until they started to be replaced by diesel in 1952. In 1954 Queen Elizabeth II toured Victoria on a train hauled by a B class diesel locomotive.

VICTORIAN RAILWAYS

Victorian Railways was established in 1883 and the trains of the state now mostly operate on government-owned 1,600 mm (5 foot 3 inch) gauge track although standard gauge 1,435 mm (4 foot 8½ inch) is used for interstate services. There are just over 4,000 (2,485 miles) of railway track in the state.

V/Line is responsible for regional diesel train services through-out the state, while freight services are now operated by several private companies. Freight trains are important for transporting various grains especially from the wheat-growing districts of the west and the north-west to coastal ports from where they are processed or exported.

One of the most famous trains was the *Spirit of Progress* between Melbourne and Albury (and on to Sydney), which commenced its air-conditioned service in 1937. In 1962, the break of gauge at Albury was eliminated by extending the standard gauge between the two state capitals. New South Wales TrainLink now operates the XPT train between Melbourne and Sydney, while the private company, Great Southern Rail, operates the service between Melbourne and Adelaide.

TRAIN SPOTTING

There are several great rail journeys in or through Victoria with the Adelaide to Melbourne and Melbourne to Sydney being two of Australia's most renowned. Train enthusiasts help retain the state's rail heritage with trains such as *Puffing Billy* being one of the biggest tourist attractions in Victoria.

Walhalla Goldfields Railway operates in this small mining town east of Melbourne near Traralgon. Services between Moe and Walhalla commenced in 1904 on an experimental 762 mm (2 foot 6 inch) railway but had closed by 1954. Now the railway company operates trains that carry tourists along a section of the Erica to Walhalla line on most weekends and public holidays.

Closer to Melbourne, the Bellarine Railway does the same on a branch line situated on the Bellarine Peninsula between Queenscliff

and Drysdale south of Melbourne. The line opened in 1879 but closed to passenger services in 1931, then closed altogether in 1976.

On the other side of Port Phillip Bay, the Mornington Railway offers another heritage steam train experience. It uses a K class steam locomotive, diesel locomotives and heritage carriages on its journey from Moorooduc to Mornington; a travelling time of just 17 minutes.

Another volunteer-operated, not-for-profit tourist train is run by the Yarra Valley Railway, based in the very popular and famous vineyard region of Victoria just out of Melbourne. Using the former Victorian Railways Yarra Glen to Healesville branch line, the train departs from Healesville and travels a short distance to Tunnel Hill and back using a Walker M22 class rail motor. Trains depart every hour from 10 a.m. until 4 p.m. on Sundays, most public holidays and from Wednesday to Sunday during the school holidays. The Yarra Valley Railway also has a collection of locomotives and rolling stock, and eventually plans to reopen the line through to Yarra Glen.

Above: Victoria has several grand and impressive railway stations including Ballarat, which was constructed to service the city's booming goldfields.

Opposite: Melbourne's iconic Flinders Street Station is located at the intersection with Swanson Street and backs onto the Yarra River.

MELBOURNE TO SYDNEY

INTERCAPITAL EXPRESS

The XPT-operated by New South Wales TrainLink connects the two largest Australian state capital cities of Sydney and Melbourne, which are 960 km (600 miles) apart. Day and night services are offered in each direction to combine trains on the New South Wales Main Southern Line to Albury with trains on Victoria's North East Line. While the cities were connected by rail in 1883, it wasn't until 1962 that a through train was possible with the opening of a standard gauge track all the way from Sydney south to Melbourne (the line was, up until then, broad gauge through Victoria from Albury to Melbourne). Trains that have operated on the track include the *Southern Aurora*, *Spirit of Progress* and the *Intercapital Daylight*.

There have been discussions about a high-speed train along this route but no definite plans have yet been put in place.

THE TRAIN

Northbound XPT trains depart from platform one of the Southern Cross Centre on Swanson Street. The tracks on which these trains

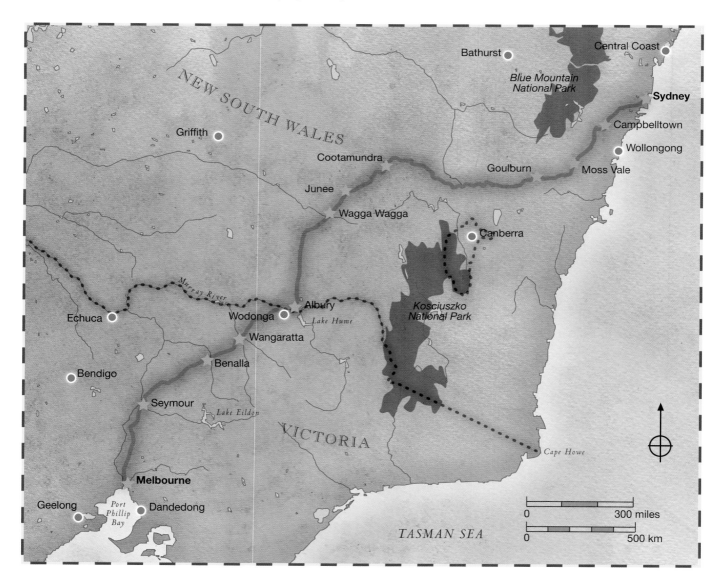

operate are managed by the Australian Rail Track Corporation.

The XPT train uses a five carriage configuration (six cars during peak holiday periods). Car A (the rear of the train from Melbourne to Sydney) is the first-class sleeper car with 18 berths (nine compartments with up and down sleeping), Car B (first class, 56 seats), Car C (first class, 21 seats, plus the buffet), Car D (economy, 68 seats), and Car E (economy, 48 seats, and luggage compartment). Sleeper beds are only available on the night train with the first-class compartments sold as individual sit-up seats on the day train.

Snacks and beverages are sold in the café of the buffet car. Alcohol is also sold in the café and only liquor purchased on the train can be consumed. Passengers are allowed to enjoy their own food and non-alcoholic beverages whilst on the train.

THE JOURNEY

There are two services: the day service (departs Melbourne at 8.30 a.m. and Sydney at 7.32 a.m.) and the night service (departs Melbourne at 7.50 p.m. and Sydney at 8.32 p.m.) with both taking approximately 11.5 hours to reach their destination. From Melbourne the train stops at the Victorian stations of Broadmeadows, Seymour, Benalla and Wangaratta. It then continues on to stop in New South Wales at Albury, Culcairn, Henty, The Rock, Wagga Wagga, Junee, Cootamundra, Harden, Yass Junction, Gunning, Goulburn, Moss Vale, Campbelltown and Sydney Central. Audio announcements are made prior to the train approaching the next station.

Almost 100 km (62 miles) north, the train stops at Seymour, which is the base for the Seymour Railway Heritage Centre. This centre has both its own trains as well as some on loan from government railways. It uses this rolling stock to operate special passenger trains thoughout the state or even interstate. Its depot, served by both broad and standard gauge tracks, is located in the heart of Seymour. It runs occasional charters to destinations such as Geelong, Echuca, Bendigo and Tocumwal as well as special trains like the *Spirit of Progress* (originally a premier express train from Melbourne to Sydney from 1937 until 1986).

Above: Northbound trains for Sydney depart from Melbourne's Southern Cross Centre.

While the train doesn't stop at Glenrowan, the town has a special place in Australian folklore as it was near here that the notorious bushrangers Ned Kelly and his gang died after a fiery shoot out with the law.

Three hours into the journey, the train stops at Wangaratta located at the junction of the King and Ovens Rivers. It is situated near Beechworth where gold was discovered in 1852 and thus became an important service centre for those working the goldfields. The railway from Sydney reached the town in 1883. It is now a convenient station for accessing the 'liquid gold' produced in the nearby wine regions of Milawa (south-east), Rutherglen (north) and the King Valley (south).

Bowser, just north of Wangaratta was previously the junction for trains on the branch lines eastward to Everton, Yackandandah, Myrtleford and Bright. The line to Bright closed in 1983 and in the 1990s, the land along the former track became the Murray to Mountains Rail Trail with Wangaratta now being a popular starting or finishing point for cyclists using this popular trail.

After crossing the Murray River the train enters New South Wales and stops at Albury, which was connected to Sydney by rail in 1883. Attractions here include the art gallery, botanic gardens,

Above right: Albury Station on the New South Wales-Victorian border was erected in 1882 and is one of the grandest railway stations in New South Wales.

Right: The journey between Melbourne and Sydney mostly passes through agricultural land.

Opposite: The train terminates at Sydney's Central Station with connections to other forms of public transport like ferries at train stations such as Circular Quay.

river cruises, riverside walks and the Ettamogah Wildlife Sanctuary. The twin towns of Albury and Wodonga are a gateway to a region that includes Lake Hume to the east, alpine valley and the historic villages of Beechworth and Yackandandah (south), the famous wineries of Rutherglen (west), and the rolling plains and quaint villages of Holbrook and Culcairn (north). It is a large region and train travellers can only access these locations via alternative transport such as a car.

Culcairn is the next stop in New South Wales with the now distinctive orange and white signboards on the station. In 1880, the new railway line from Sydney reached Henty, which had been settled by German families who had trekked overland from South Australia. Grain crops are all-important in this part of Australia and their success owes a lot to a former Henty farmer named Headlie Taylor who, in 1914, invented the header harvester. This machine harvested wheat more efficiently than before and assisted in the bulk handling of wheat in Australia and elsewhere.

The Rock is a small train junction town for a branch line that heads to the south-west and the towns of Lockhart, Boree Creek, Urana and Oaklands. It remains partially open and is used for the transportation of grain.

Other important stops along the route include Wagga Wagga (the state's largest inland city) and Junee where the locomotive drivers change (the onboard crew changes at Albury). The Sydney to Griffith XPT service also passes through Junee on its journey westward to Griffith.

Yass Junction is the next stop and the junction for a now-closed branch line that once continued into Yass. In 1892, the railway from Sydney arrived in the town of Yass with the original station building (not Yass Junction) now home to the Yass Railway Heritage Centre. Yass is renowned as a famous merino wool-producing district while Murrumbateman, just to the south, is developing as an important wine region with its boutique wineries offering cellardoor tastings to visitors.

While it is possible to travel to Canberra via direct rail services from Sydney (see page 82), the connection from Melbourne requires a combination of train and coach with the preferred stop for joining the coach being Yass Junction (Cootamundra is another possibility but not the quicker of the two).

Few passengers alight here, most head northwards to Goulburn, then to the Southern Highlands, Moss Vale and Bowral (see page 66) before reaching Sydney Central.

PUFFING BILLY

GEM OF THE HILLS

This relic from the past, one of Australia's favourite railways, entered service with the Victorian Railways in 1900 to carry passengers and goods (timber and potatoes in particular) through the mountainous district between Upper Ferntree Gully and Gembrook located to the east of Melbourne.

By 1930, the line was already recognized as a liability to the state railway and due to a landslide in 1953, the decision was made to close it in 1954. Not one to be disregarded though, a preservation society was formed and the line reopened in 1962. It has since carried millions of new-found passengers from all around the globe (it averages over 400,000 passengers per annum). Tourist services resumed between Belgrave and Menzies Creek in 1962, then extended to Emerald in 1965, Lakeside in 1975 and Gembrook in 1998.

Nobody seems to know how the name *Puffing Billy* came about but everyone knows this excursion train to be one of Melbourne's most appealing tourism attractions.

Today, *Puffing Billy* is one of the finest preserved steam railways in the world. It commenced operations in 1900 and operates on every day of the year except Christmas Day. Its return journey from Belgrave to Lakeside covers 26 km (16 miles) through towering eucalypt forests, tree fern-lined gullies, rolling farmland and small acreage residential properties of the Dandenong Ranges.

One of the big attractions is that many people, young and old, enjoy in safety the possibility of extending their legs over the side of the open-sided train (with protective railing) travelling at no more than 24 km/h (15 mph).

Admiring the route at different times of the year is another appeal as there can be dramatic changes in the weather and the colours of the foliage. Enjoy a myriad of autumnal hues and the crisp, misty atmosphere of winter. Though rare, a light dusting of snow is possible in winter, while in summer, the shaded glens and streams offer a cool respite from the heat.

This not-for-profit train, operated by the Emerald Tourist Railway Board in conjunction with the *Puffing Billy* Preservation Society, employs some 65 full-time staff supplemented by the dedicated efforts of over 900 volunteers. Member discounts are available plus they receive a quarterly magazine.

Various excursion trains also operate in addition to the scheduled services. These include special trains, such as 'Steam and Cuisine' (After Dark and Luncheon trains offering various menu options), 'Murder on the *Puffing Billy* Express', 'Dine and Dance' (with dancing done in the Nobelius Packing Shed) and 'Rhythm and Blues', that combine the train journey, meals,

Opposite: For much of its journey *Puffing Billy* passes through fern-lined gullies that thrive beneath towering eucalyptus trees.

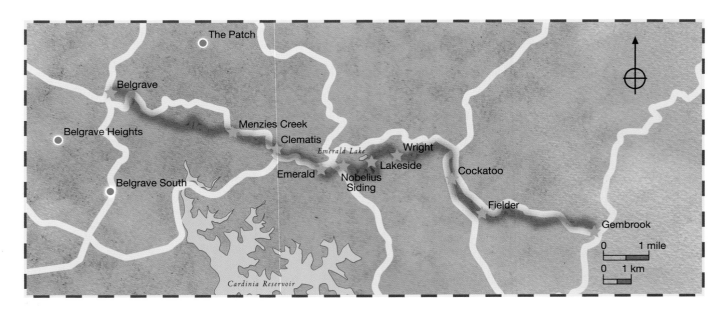

drinks and entertainment. The Great Train Race attracts over 3,500 runners who try to beat the train over a 13.5-km (8½-mile) section of the track. Special dinner trains operate using four restored heritage dining cars that seat up to 22 passengers. Trains are also available for special interest charters. 'A Day Out with Thomas' activities are held during autumn and spring at Gembrook Station.

A *Puffing Billy* Railway Museum at Menzies Creek is planned.

THE TRAIN

The Belgrave to Gembrook line was one of four experimental narrow gauge lines (760 mm / 2 foot 6 inch) opened to help develop some rural parts of Victoria. Only two remain with the Walhalla Goldfields Railway being the other.

The Baldwin steam locomotive was designed in the United States, and it is to this design that five of *Puffing Billy*'s locomotives were built at the Newport Workshops in Victoria. The railway operations are supplemented by three diesel locomotives (one previously operated in Tasmania and the other two in Queensland) usually on days of total fire bans. The steam locomotives are painted in different colours and numbered 6A (black), 7A (Canadian red), 8A (green), 12A (Canadian red) and 14A (black).

Various restored heritage carriages are hauled by the locomotive and feature open sides with protective railings, as well as informative guides and maps of the route. Both first- and second-class coaches operate but there is no differentiation in pricing or passenger comfort.

THE JOURNEY

Most *Puffing Billy* journeys start in Belgrave 42 km (26 miles) from Melbourne with electric Melbourne Metro trains taking just over one hour to cover the distance (the steam train station is a short walk from the Metro Station; follow the blue line on the footpath).

Various travel options are available with most passengers travelling on the Belgrave-Lakeside-Belgrave service that takes about three hours.

Belgrave Station is normally a hive of activity prior to the train's departure with trains being shunted and refuelled at the locomotive running shed and workshop, and passengers refuelling themselves at the well-stocked platform restroom and souvenir shop.

Not long after departure the train crosses the iconic 15-span, Monbulk Creek trestle bridge (91 m/300 ft), which is suitably curved to enable good photography especially from the rear, right-hand side of the train. The train passes through parts of Sherbrooke Forest dominated by majestic stands of towering mountain ash eucalypts (the world's tallest flowering plant) with an understorey of luxuriant tree ferns.

Menzies Creek Station, 30 minutes from Belgrave, is the first stop and a place where trains often cross. Continuing, the train passes through Clematis Station and the Paradise Hotel before pulling into Emerald Station, the highest station on the line and a railway repair yard.

Nobelius Packing Shed, a venue for 'Dine and Dance' trains is passed before the train pulls into Lakeside. Here, the steam train takes on water while passengers alight and can take in the views of Emerald Lake Park or even walk the trails and picnic here before taking a later train back to Belgrave.

Passengers who continue on the Gembrook train will pass through Wright, Cockatoo and Fielder before reaching the former timber town of Gembrook. The train stops here for one hour for passengers to explore the historic town.

Daily departures from Belgrave to Lakeside leave at 10.30 a.m., 12.30 p.m. and 2.30 p.m. with a one-hour stop allocated at Lakeside Station. The Belgrave to Gembrook service departs at 11.10 a.m. and arrives back at Belgrave at 3.30 p.m. The service is affected by total fire bans when a diesel locomotive replaces the steam train (fire patrol officers also follow each train in a vehicle converted for operating on the railway). Adult, child, concession, group (20 or more) and family rates apply (two adults pay and four kids travel free).

Above: Several wooden trestle bridges are crossed.

Opposite: The repositioning of the steam locomotive at Belgrave Station provides an opportunity for photographs.

MELBOURNE TO BALLARAT

A CITY BUILT BY GOLD

Ballarat on the banks of the Yarrowee River is a major regional city in Victoria of 100,000 residents, 110 km (68 miles) north-west of Melbourne with a travelling time from there on V/Line trains of 86 minutes.

Ballarat and many other towns and villages in this part of Victoria owe their existence to the discovery of gold in the 1850s. In 1851, gold was unearthed in Clunes in central Victoria and within three months over 8,000 miners had descended on the tranquil rural district. They came from England, the Californian goldfields and China. So important was gold in this part of the world that when Mark Twain visited Ballarat in 1895 he commented: "It was as if the name Ballarat had suddenly been written on the sky, where all the world could read it at once."

By 1852, the population of Ballarat had swollen to 30,000 and by 1855 there were 100,000 miners on goldfields scattered throughout the Victoria. The miners were like locusts swarming over the landscape in an effort to stake out their claim. Initially makeshift dwellings and shops opened to provide essential tools and supplies.

In 1869, the world-famous and largest surface nugget ever unearthed, the 'Welcome Stranger' was found in Moliagul near Ballarat (estimated to be 71 kg/157 lb). Gold is still to be found

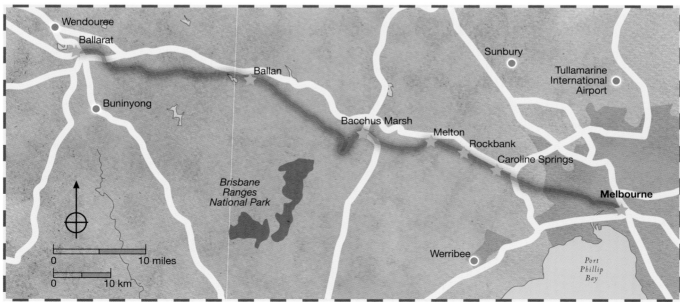

but not in the same proportions, though in 1980 the 27.2 kg (60 lb) 'Hand of Faith' nugget was unearthed and sold to the Golden Nugget Casino in Las Vegas.

With its newfound wealth, the residents of Ballarat called on the government to establish a rail link. Work on the Geelong to Ballarat line commenced in 1858 (a rail line from Melbourne to Geelong was already in existence). The broad-gauge line arrived in Ballarat in 1862 and remained as the main rail link to Melbourne until a more direct line between Ballarat and the capital opened in 1889.

Ballarat has also played an important role with Victorian Railways through the Ballarat North Workshop located here. This opened in 1917 as a repair and maintenance workshop but from 1919 to 1922 some steam trains were built here. In the 1960s, goods wagons were also built and by the 1980s work commenced on repairing and maintaining Melbourne's electric trains and trams.

Ballarat is ideal as a day-visit destination by train while there are many reasons for spending a longer time here. For those who are interested in the city's grand buildings, it is possible to set off on foot from the train station to take in the main city centre attractions. Guided heritage tours of the historic town centre are conducted twice daily.

THE TRAIN

A Bombardier diesel train of up to ten carriages operates on this line and offers a smooth and fast ride. Carriages are quiet (there are dedicated quiet cars too where passengers are required to minimize any noise); just one class is offered. The seating arrangement is double seats on either side of the aisle. Audio announcements and digital signs herald the next station.

Above: V/Line trains for Ballarat depart from Melbourne's Southern Cross Centre.

Opposite: The discovery of gold enabled the erection of many grand buildings in Ballarat including the impressive clock tower of the Ballarat Railway Station.

THE JOURNEY

Ballarat trains depart Melbourne's Southern Cross Centre and head north-west towards Ballarat and the Victorian goldfields. These trains stop at Footscray, Sunshine, Ardeer, Deer Park, Caroline Springs, Rockbank, Melton, Bacchus Marsh and Ballan before terminating at either Ballarat or Wendouree.

At Caroline Springs and 20 minutes into the journey, the train is already in open farmland and shortly after in Rockbank, the landscape is dominated by farms. The train may make an extended stop at Melton while it waits for the train heading towards Melbourne to clear the single track line.

Rolling agricultural land and eucapypt forests extend from here to Ballarat with a large horse studfarm passed just after Ballan. Horse racing has always been a feature of Melbourne life – the Melbourne Cup on the first Tuesday in November is a Victorian public holiday. Considered one of the richest horse races in the world, it now attracts entries from around the globe. Michelle Payne, the first female jockey ever to win a Melbourne Cup lives just outside Ballarat.

Trains arrive at Ballarat's grand 19th-century station located on Lydiard North Street from the south-east. The full grandeur of the station is revealed after passengers have stepped out of the two-platform station and looked backwards. The original station (known as Ballarat West before the station at Ballarat East closed) was constructed in 1862 but many of the striking features were only added in 1891 after the direct service to Melbourne was opened in 1889. These included a stationmaster's office, grand portico and the impressive clock tower.

While a fire in 1981 destroyed some features, most were restored and now much of historic interior remains in place. The station's refreshment rooms are impressive and popular with commuters and travellers.

Ballarat has several tourist attractions such as Sovereign Hill (a themed and working gold mine) and the Museum of Australian Democracy at Eureka just a little out of the city centre. What is commonly called the Battle of the Eureka Stockade occurred in 1854 when miners revolted against British colonial rule. A battle ensued between the rebels and soldiers with 27 deaths, mostly rebels. The incident is considered to be the birth of Australian democracy because in 1856 white males received the vote.

Ballarat's central business district is compact and well worth exploring on foot. Its grand architecture reflects a town built on

gold. The Art Gallery of Ballarat has arguably the country's best regional collection of Australian art ranging from 1887 to contemporary.

Some of the other grand buildings in the city include Her Majesty's Theatre, Regent Theatre and the old post office (now the Federation University and Ballarat's significant second art gallery). Her Majesty's Theatre opened in 1875 and is acknowledged as Australia's best-preserved theatre building. Another grand building of interest is Craig's Royal Hotel on Lydiard Street where Prince Alfred, Duke of Edinburgh stayed in 1867 on what was the first visit to Australia by a royal. Interestingly, some months later a Ballarat resident named Henry O'Farrell attempted Australia's first political assassination when he shot Prince Alfred who was officiating at a function in Sydney.

When these grand buildings opened, the town was also served by a horse-drawn, double-deck tramway with the main track running in front of the Town Hall. The Ballarat Tramway Museum, operated by volunteers, has a sizable collection of Ballarat trams, which serviced the city from 1887 to 1971. These and trams from other parts of the state operate around the Botanical Gardens beside Lake Wendouree.

Visitors to Ballarat may also be interested in sightseeing around Lake Wendouree, visiting the Gold Museum, Botanical Gardens and the Gold Exchange on Lydiard Street South.

The rail line continues a little beyond Ballarat to suburban Wendouree while trains to Aarat and Horsham also pass through Ballarat. The line westward from Ballarat towards Aarat is often referred to as the Serviceton Line as it once connected to Serviceton on the Victoria-South Australia border (see Adelaide to Melbourne train, page 28).

Just to the west of the city, the former Ballarat to Skipton railway line is now disused and has been converted into a 53-km (33-mile) rail trail. This line operated between 1883 and 1985 as a link between the gold towns west of Ballarat and the surrounding pastoral district including the towns of Scarsdale (line opened in 1883) and Linton (opened 1891).

Above: A train journey here enables visitors to walk the streets of Ballarat's city centre lined with historic buildings, such as the Mining Exchange.

Opposite: Relive the gold rush days at Sovereign Hill; just a short taxi ride away from the railway station.

MELBOURNE TO SWAN HILL

CITY TO THE BUSH

This service links Melbourne with Swan Hill located beside Australia's longest river, the Murray. Swan Hill lies 335 km (208 miles) north-west of Melbourne on the border with New South Wales. It is a service centre and port for the surrounding farms where crops are grown, sheep graze, and vegetables and vines thrive.

THE TRAIN

This five-carriage train is hauled by a diesel locomotive with the first three carriages offering unreserved economy-class seating, the fourth car is for reserved economy and a buffet, and the last carriage has reserved first-class seating (the configuration is reversed on the return journey after the locomotive is relocated from one end to the other).

Seating in first class is a four-seat configuration (60 seats in total); two either side of the aisle, while in economy, it is three and two seats separated by an aisle (88 seats per carriage). Luggage can be stored in above-seat racks while large bags maybe stored in the baggage compartment, which also has facilities for bicycles.

Hot and cold snacks and beverages are sold and, while it's not gourmet dining, the shelves and fridges are stacked with sandwiches, pies, cakes and muffins. Brewed coffee and cold drinks are sold but there is no alcohol available.

THE JOURNEY

This service, operated by V/Line, departs from Melbourne's Southern Cross Centre at 7.41 a.m. and stops at Water Gardens, Sunbury, Gisborne, Woodend, Kyneton, Castlemaine, Bendigo, Eaglehawk, Woodvale, Dingee, Pyramid and Kerang before terminating at Swan Hill.

The landscape is already semi-rural by the time the train reaches Sunbury. On the right on leaving Sunbury the mansion that can be seen is called Rupertswood, built in 1874 by William (later, Sir William) Clarke. It had its own railway station for shipping hay bales to Adelaide but it was bypassed when the track was upgraded. Clarke was the president of the Melbourne Cricket Club, and in 1882 a touring English cricket team visited and played a local team. After the match, Lady Clarke took some bails from the stumps, burnt them and placed the ashes in a pouch before presenting them to the English captain. This lead to the famous Ashes (now in an

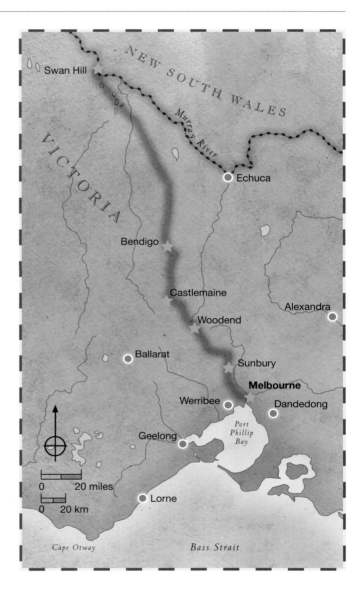

urn), which has become the perpetual trophy for matches played between Australia and England.

Further on, passengers for Daylesford with its mineral waters and wellness centres, change at Woodend for their coach transfer.

Castlemaine has an old wooden stationhouse where passengers for Maryborough and Malden join an awaiting coach. Others alight for the Castlemaine Goldfields Railway, which operates on Wednesdays, Sundays, school holidays, some Saturdays and public holidays.

Just a little over two hours into the journey, the Sacred Heart Cathedral Bendigo spire appears before the train arrives into the city. Bendigo is a vibrant city with beautiful streets that are the legacy of the gold rush. Sights include the Art Gallery, Town Hall, Performing Arts Centre, Bendigo Pottery, Golden Dragon Museum (a celebration of the region's Chinese history) and a vintage tram that travels along historic streetscapes.

Next stop is Eaglehawk, once a mining town, then on to Pyramid, after which the scenery is mostly broad-acre sheep grazing land with patches of eucalyptus trees. At Kerang, passengers for Shepperaton and Albury leave the train to continue their journey on an awaiting coach.

While the train does not stop at Lake Boga, it is worth returning here via car from Swan Hill for the Lake Boga Flying Boat Museum, which showcases where Catalina flying boats were repaired under a shroud of mystery during the Second World War.

Swan Hill is a modern town with its city centre close to the station on Curlewis Street, in front of Riverside Park and the southern banks of the Murray River. The statue outside the station is called the Big Cod. The giant murray cod is Australia's largest freshwater fish and though not as plentiful as before, it is still a

prized catch. While this is mostly sheep and wheat country, there are several wineries around Swan Hill and further downstream the wineries of Mildura thrive.

Above: The diesel locomotive is repositioned from the front of the train to the rear at Swan Hill.

Below: A short walk from the railway station, Swan Hill's Pioneer Settlement offers a window onto the past.

NEW SOUTH WALES

INTRODUCTION

Sydney, Australia's largest and oldest city, has a comprehensive urban rail network and is the departure and arrival point for many train journeys throughout the state. The nation's pioneering state covers 801,600 sq km (309,500 sq miles) or 10.5 per cent of the total country.

Sydney Central Station is where the famous *Indian Pacific* starts and ends its journey. Other rail journeys head to other parts of the state such as the Blue Mountains, Dubbo, Armidale and Bomaderry as well as interstate to Brisbane, Adelaide (via Broken Hill) and Melbourne.

Australia's first railway is thought to be that opened in Newcastle, New South Wales, by the Australian Agricultural Company, which in 1831 operated an inclined plane railway to transport coal from a colliery on the hill above the settlement down to the docks at the mouth of the Hunter River. The coal was loaded into wagons and pushed along rail tracks down the hill using gravity and human power.

The state's first public railway commenced operations from Sydney to Granville (east of Parramatta) in 1855; now an extensive passenger and freight train network on 1,440 mm (4 foot 8½ inch) gauge rail covers a large area of Sydney and the state.

New South Wales TrainLink, operated by NSW Trains, provides the train and coach services that connect regional centres throughout the state to Sydney as well as Canberra, Brisbane and Melbourne. It also provides intercity train services between Sydney and the Central Coast, Newcastle, the Lower Hunter, the Blue Mountains, Lithgow, Bathurst, the South Coast and Southern Highlands. Seats on regional trains and coaches need to be pre-booked online, by phone or over the counter. Ticket prices vary only for full adult fares throughout the year depending upon peak, shoulder or low season.

One of the most recent changes to the Sydney train network is the introduction of the Opal Card, a pre-loaded card using smart-card technology, which is now required for travel on bus, train, ferry and light rail travel transport in Sydney, the Blue Mountains, Central Coast, Hunter, Illawarra and Southern Highlands. Visitors can purchase the card and use it on Sydney's suburban network to travel, for example, to Circular Quay to see the origins of

Australian European settlement around the foreshore and the adjoining Rocks district located below the iconic Sydney Harbour Bridge and opposite the equally famous, sail-like structure of the Sydney Opera House. Trains to Sydney's North Shore cross the Harbour Bridge on its western side.

NSW TrainLink offers a Discovery Pass (adult and child, economy and premium) for those who want to travel to 365 regional destinations across New South Wales, Victoria, Queensland and the Australian Capital Territory for periods of travel between two weeks to six months.

Byron Bay Railroad Company is a not-for-profit group that operates a short rail service in northern New South Wales. While just a 3 km (1.9 mile) service, it is significant as it is reportedly the world's first solar-powered train. It operates between Northbeach Station at Sunrise Beach in front of Elements of Byron Resort and the Byron Beach platform adjacent to the Shirley Street level crossing. The two-carriage, 600 class railcar was built at Chullora Railway Workshop in Sydney in 1949. It operates along part of the 132-km (82-mile) Casino to Murwillumbah line. There were once 32 stations along this stretch of railway until all services were

suspended in 2004. The conversion of the diesel railcars took place at the Lithgow State Mine Railway where the heritage railcar has been stored for some 14 years. The original plan for the railway was to operate the train as a diesel service but the decision was made to convert to solar power.

Regular heritage train services such as the Cockatoo Run to Robertson and Moss Vale plus the Hawkesbury River Express to Hawkesbury River and Gosford are operated by 3801 Limited, a not-for-profit group of train enthusiasts.

The Zig Zag Heritage Railway was severely damaged by bush-fire in 2013 with substantial amounts of infrastructure destroyed or damaged. Teams of volunteers have been working tirelessly

to reopen the railway. Located to the east of Lithgow, this is an engineering masterpiece dating back to the 1860s and involving a number of intricate switchbacks.

Transport Heritage NSW Ltd is a not-for-profit, member-based organisation that incorporates the activities of the former NSW Rail Transport Museum, Trainworks Limited and the Office of Rail Heritage. It operates museums at Thirlmere and Valley Heights, and conducts heritage train journeys throughout the state.

Above: The solar-powered Byron Bay Railway is a recent edition to the railway journeys offered in New South Wales.

Opposite: Train departures are listed on the destination board within the impressive concourse of Sydney Central Station.

SYDNEY TO BRISBANE

HARBOURSIDE TO RIVERSIDE

The North Coast line connects the New South Wales capital of Sydney to the Queensland capital of Brisbane thus linking one of the world's most scenic harbours with one of the most world's most scenic riverside cities.

The coastal stretch from Sydney northwards to Tweed Heads in northern New South Wales and on to the Gold Coast in southern Queensland is one Australia's most popular holiday coastlines. Coastal towns and regions from the south to the north along this train journey include the Central Coast, Port Stephens, Forster Tuncurry, Port Macquarie, Coffs Harbour, Yamba and Byron Bay. Some of these are close to the railway although the train does head away from the coast at Coffs Harbour to travel via Grafton, Casino and Kyogle in inland northern New South Wales before arriving into Brisbane.

Northern departures on this XPT service of 1,100 km (684 miles) depart Sydney Central for Brisbane at 2.41 p.m. Arrival times into Brisbane differ during summer as Queensland, which does not implement daylight saving, is one hour behind New South Wales which does (arrival time into Brisbane's Roma Street is normally 4.53 a.m. but is 3.53 a.m., in summer). This means that passengers on this service will travel in the dark from about Gloucester northwards. The alternative for those wishing to view the countryside, is to travel this route in reverse departing Brisbane at 5.55 a.m. (4.55 a.m. during daylight saving) and arriving into Sydney Central that evening at 8.12 p.m. Another possibility for those wishing to admire the scenery of northern New South Wales is to travel on the daily XPT service to Casino (departing Sydney Central at 7.11 a.m. and arriving in Casino at 6.41 p.m.) and then join the train to Brisbane when it passes through Casino at 2.19 a.m. the next morning.

THE TRAIN

Passengers have three seating options with economy, first class and first-class sleepers available. The North Coast train is one of a few in the state that provides first-class sleepers, tickets for which are sold at a premium. Car A at the front of the train is the sleeping car with just nine compartments accommodating two sleeping passengers each. However, when the train operates as a day train, three passengers may be accommodated in each compartment.

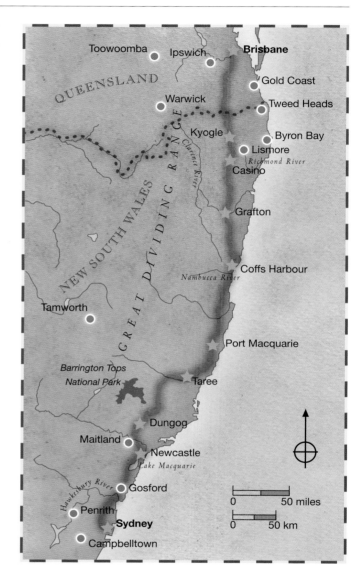

Alternate sleeping compartments face in different directions, so passengers with issues about travelling backwards need to carefully select their seat when making a booking should they opt for a sleeper (bookings for sleepers have to be made in person at a railway station). Seats one to three face backwards and seats five to seven are forward facing (for some reason, there is no seat four). This sequence continues through to seats 33 to 35, which

Opposite: This train provides a connection to several coastal beachside destinations like Coffs Harbour and near-deserted beaches just to the north.

face backwards. Two compartments share a combined shower and toilet located between them. Passengers in first-class sleepers are issued with a towel and an amenities kit containing soap, shampoo, toothbrush and toothpaste. They also receive a complimentary welcome snack and drink pack and, in the morning, breakfast of coffee/tea, muesli, milk, juice and toast before the train arrives into Brisbane. Linen sheets, two pillows and a blanket ensure a comfortable sleep.

Normal first-class and economy class seating is the same as on other XPT trains.

THE JOURNEY

The North Coast service proceeds from Sydney to Maitland on the same section of the line as the train to Armidale (see page 68) but deviates to the north just after with stops at Dungog, Gloucester, Wingham, Taree, Kendall, Wauchope, Kempsey, Eungai, Macksville, Nambucca Heads, Urunga, Sawtell, Coffs Harbour, Grafton, Casino and Kyogle.

On the Central Coast the track crosses the expansive Hawkesbury River, skirts the scenic waterways before Gosford, then routes around the western side of Lake Macquarie before arriving at Broadmeadow, which is now the main station for those alighting at Newcastle. The line continues north from Maitland to Dungog and Gloucester through lush green pasturelands where contented dairy and beef cattle graze.

The track then passes on the eastern side of the vast wilderness of temperate rainforests and wild rivers known as Barrington Tops National Park where snow occasionally falls during winter. From here, the line continues north into the Manning Valley and the towns of Wingham and Taree. Australia's highest waterfall drop of 120 m (394 ft) is located at Ellenborough just out of Taree.

Wauchope is the next stop and while quiet now, it once had a busy goods yard for the shipping of timber logged from surrounding forests. At one stage, Wauchope was Australia's biggest timber town and Timbertown, a heritage theme park on the outskirts of the town, celebrates the role of this commodity in the local community. There is a steam train here, as well as Cobb and Co stagecoach and bullock carts. Passengers for Port Macquarie alight from the train in Wauchope.

Kempsey is another inland town along the route, 345 km (215 miles) north of Sydney. Located on the Macleay River it, too, has a long history of logging especially for the much-prized red

cedar. Dairying is now important with several cheese and butter factories in the region. Nestlé Milo was invented in Australia and first made in nearby Smithtown.

The town of Macksville, on the Nambucca River, is halfway between Sydney and Brisbane. A little further along is Nambucca Heads near the mouth of the river and a popular holiday destination.

Coffs Harbour is one of the state's largest coastal holiday destinations especially for families. After this stop, the train makes a distinctive turn inland on its way to Grafton beside the banks of the Clarence River and located some 35 km (22 miles) from the coast. The bridge over the Clarence is of interest as it is double-decker with the train track on the lower level and motor vehicles above.

Casino on the banks of the Richmond River is also located inland. The beef industry is important to the town, which has positioned itself as Australia's beef capital. It is also the terminus station for the daily Sydney to Casino XPT train and there is a disused branch line heading north-east from Casino that once served the towns of Lismore and Murwillumbah.

However, the Brisbane service continues northwards towards Kyogle on the Richmond River and the Queensland border.

Kyogle is the stop for Nimbin (20 km / 12 miles away), which, in the 1970s, became the epicentre for alternative and counter-cultural lifestylers who moved there and established communes to farm the land and to produce artisanal craft products. Many remain in the surrounding district and Nimbin's Rainbow Café is an essential stop in the town.

The train journeys north through the Border Ranges National Park located on the border between New South Wales and Queensland. This park is home to two important railway features known as the Spiral Loop and Border Loop, which were necessary for trains to cross over the high mountain range between the two states. Both are part of the first standard gauge railway linking two Australian state capitals with the project initiated after the First World War to create employment for returning soldiers. Walks and lookouts within the park enable dedicated trainspotters the opportunity to view trains negotiating both loops.

Above: Passengers from the Hunter Valley can board the train at Broadmeadow Station.

Opposite: The train travels northward across the picturesque Hawkesbury River, then snakes its way around Brisbane Water.

SYDNEY TO THE BLUE MOUNTAINS AND THE SCENIC RAILWAY

HEAD FOR THE HILLS AND THE VALLEYS BELOW

The railway westward from Sydney to Katoomba and on to Lithgow is one of Australia's busiest with commuter trains operated by NSW TrainLink (parts of this organisation once operated as RailCorp, CountryLink and CityRail) as well as freight trains (mostly coal) traversing what is the Main Western Line. The Western Line from Sydney reached Parramatta in 1855 and the first railway to the mountains was from Penrith to Weatherboard (Wentworth Falls) in 1867.

Trains to the Blue Mountains depart hourly from Sydney's Central Station with its majestic clock tower. There were two earlier stations prior to the current honey-coloured sandstone building, which was opened in 1906. The clock tower was added in 1921. Central's grand concourse has ten main platforms and is also the departure point for other great railway journeys such as the *Indian Pacific* (see page 18) and destinations like Armidale, Dubbo, Melbourne, Canberra and Brisbane.

Opposite: The terminus for the Katoomba Scenic World railway is a minute splash of red within its forest and cliff surroundings.

MOUNTAINOUS ESCAPADES

Katoomba is the main town in the Blue Mountains and is two hours (122 km/75 miles) to the west of Sydney. Situated on a dissected sandstone plateau, its near-vertical escarpment presented an impenetrable barrier to European settlers but in 1813, three adventurers named Blaxland, Wentworth and Lawson identified a route and were rewarded with three towns here named after them. In doing so, the explorers opened up fertile pasturelands inland from the Blue Mountains. The journey to cooler destinations like Katoomba (altitude 1,017 m/3,336 ft above sea level) was popular and several towns became affordable holiday destinations for Sydneysiders.

Hotels like The Carrington in Katoomba and the Hydro Majestic in Medlow Bath became fashionable and now renovated to their former glory, they still appeal. Relaxing in cafés was a popular pastime with the opulent Art Deco-styled Paragon Café in Katoomba still maintaining the trend. Leura, Wentworth Falls, Blackheath and Mount Victoria are also popular for bushwalks.

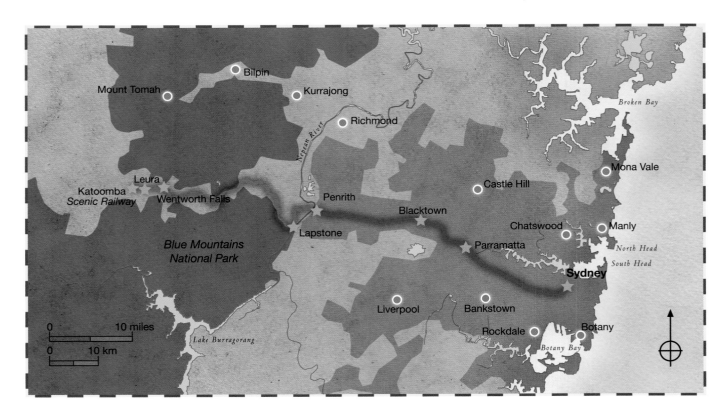

These mountains are named blue due to their colour when viewed from a distance, which scientists believe is a misty haze created by eucalyptus oil transpiring from leaves. These forests with over 100 eucalypt species cover much of the cliffs, ravines and gorges on the escarpment and plateau of what is now a UNESCO World Heritage Site.

STATIONS AND ONBOARD FACILITIES

Sydney's Central Station is the main departure point for trains to the suburbs and destinations further afield including the Blue Mountains.

Carriages of the 4, 6 or 8-car trains are double-decker with both levels accommodating approximately 80 passengers, all travelling in one class. Passengers can reverse the seats by swinging them forwards or backwards. Some carriages are quiet cars where mobile phone usage isn't encouraged.

Pre-paid Opal card tickets are mandatory on all of Sydney's public transport, although single tickets are sold at stations.

THE JOURNEY

Most trains are express trains stopping only at major stations such as Strathfield, Parramatta, Blacktown and Penrith before becoming all-stations, once they have climbed the escarpment to Lapstone and are on the plateau.

Freight trains are hauled by diesel locomotives, while all passenger trains are electric since the line was electrified in the 1950s.

Many visitors just spend the day in the mountains, although there is abundant and varied accommodation to occupy adventurous visitors and bushwalkers for several days. Day visitors should head for the mountains as early as possible and then use public buses or the local Explorer Bus to visit the main attractions as well as the townships of Leura, Katoomba and Wentworth Falls. There are several tourist sites and trails that are accessible from railway stations.

Trains continue westward from Katoomba to Lithgow and Bathurst with stops at Medlow Bath, Blackheath, Mount Victoria, Bell and Zig Zag. Zig Zag is the stop for the Zig Zag Railway, which has reopened after a disastrous 2013 bushfire destroyed sections of the track. Zig zags were once a feature on the eastern and western sides of the escarpment including one from Emu Plains to Glenbrook. To get up a near-vertical cliff, trains rise gently in one direction, then stop, disconnect the locomotive and take it to the other end of the train, then gently climb in the opposite direction. They do this several times and eventually arrive at the top.

SCENIC RAILWAY –
THE WORLD'S STEEPEST RAILWAY

An essential destination is the Scenic Railway located at Katoomba Scenic World, 3 km (nearly 2 miles) from Katoomba Station. Australia's shortest (at 310 m (1,017 ft) and reportedly the world's steepest railway (it descends into the Jamison Valley at an incline of 52 degrees) isn't just an exhilarating journey for train enthusiasts, it's also the most visited, privately-owned tourist attraction in the southern hemisphere, attracting one million tourists annually.

Besides its other accolades, with departures every ten minutes this is also the railway with Australia's most frequent timetable. This small, semi-open sided, cog-wheel railway descends at four metres (13 ft) per second from the top of the escarpment through rainforest to the valley. The decline into the Jamison Valley can be made even steeper by reclining the adjustable seats to 62 degrees for a 'cliff-hanger ride'. Its four glass-roofed carriages have a capacity of 84 passengers.

European technology powers the railway with companies such as Doppelmayr-Garaventa Group and CWA Constructions supplying the carriages and cables that guide the railway.

While purely a tourist attraction, the original tramway was constructed in 1891 to enable coal and kerosene shale to be extracted from seams within the sedimentary rock at the cliff base in the Jamison Valley. These resources were transported to the main railway line near Katoomba Station. When mining ceased in the 1930s the entrepreneurial Harry Hammon realised the potential of the railway for tourism. He incorporated seats into the two-car coal skips to carry passengers. The original 'Jessie' is still visible at the summit of the railway and Katoomba Scenic World is still owned by the Hammon Family.

Major thunderstorms are all that stop the railway from operating daily from 9 a.m. to 5 p.m. and extended to 8.30 p.m. during peak holiday periods. Snow falls once or twice during winter but this does not impact upon the operations of the railway. The railway is not suitable for those with limited mobility.

As well as the train, there is the 510-m (1,673-ft) long Scenic Cableway that gently ascends the escarpment. Its fully-enclosed cabin has panoramic windows providing aerial views of the Scenic Railway. At the top, the 720-m (2,362-ft) Scenic Skyway traverses a 270-m (886-ft) ravine where spectacular views of Katoomba Falls and the rainforest are provided through a section of glass flooring.

Right: Ride reportedly the world's steepest railway at Katoomba Scenic World.

SYDNEY TO BOWRAL

EXPLORING THE SOUTHERN TABLELANDS

The New South Wales Southern Highlands is a mostly agricultural district some 2.5 hours by train to the south-west of Sydney. The main places of interest along the way include Mittagong, Bowral, Berrima and Bundanoon.

European settlers arrived in the early 1800s and cleared much of the vegetation for grazing land, which now bears a striking resemblance to the English countryside. Wealthy, city-based families established grand country retreats and even today, while there are many farmers in the highlands, there are others who have country estates and travel here at weekends to enjoy the country lifestyle and cooler weather. Accommodation for visitors is mostly modest with intimate guesthouses being especially popular.

The railway line from Mittagong through to Moss Vale arrived in Bowral in 1867 with the original station being named Burradoo and then Bowrall (its modern spelling was adopted in 1888). Some trains continue on to Goulburn and trains to Canberra and Griffith also pass through the stations of the Southern Highlands.

Trains are not only an efficient and fast way to explore parts of the Southern Highlands but also offer excellent value for money with the use of an Opal Card.

THE TRAIN

Trains used along this part of the route are the same as those on some other Sydney metropolitan services and those on the South Coast line. They are modern, double-decker OSCAR electric trains featuring designated quiet carriages.

The Bowral service from Campbelltown is operated by a three-car Endeavour diesel train.

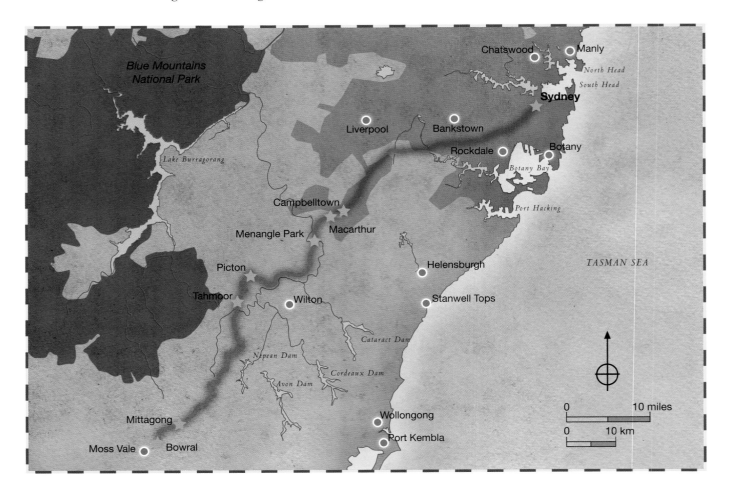

THE JOURNEY

Trains for the Southern Highlands depart from Sydney Central and head towards Macarthur. A change of train at either Campbelltown or Macarthur some one hour later is required for the Bowral service. Macarthur is named after John and Elizabeth Macarthur who were pioneer settlers and leading producers of fine wool. Both Campbelltown and Macarthur are at the edges of Sydney's urban sprawl and semi-rural in nature. The train passes Menangle Park (home to a well known race track), Picton and Tahmoor and by this stage, suburban Sydney is well behind as the line passes through the scrubby forest of Wirrimbirra Sanctuary. Mittagong, the gateway to the Southern Highlands, is the next major station and Bowral is reached just five minutes later.

Bowral is the biggest town in the Southern Highlands (population of 12,000) but popular with weekend urban landowners who travel here for the genteel rural life that also has all the city trappings of cafés, restaurants, antique shops, bookstores, and arts and craft shops.

The much-prized tulip flower has made the town famous with May and September being the best times to visit Bowral, as this is when the grand temperate gardens and leafy parks best show their colours. The Tulip Time Festival is staged annually for two weeks from mid to late September. Many travel to Bowral to inspect such parks and gardens with one of the most popular and expansive parks being the Sir Donald Bradman Oval with its adjoining Bradman Museum and International Cricket Hall of Fame. The world's most acclaimed batsman played his formative cricket and honed his skills here, so the ground is hallowed turf for those who love the noble red ball game. While many of the displays in the world-class hall pay tribute to the famous and late cricketer, there are other fascinating displays on the game itself, its origins, World Series Cricket and the greats of the game.

Some other tourist attractions in the Southern Highlands to seek out include the Australian Alpaca Centre in Berrima, the Berrima Lavender Farm and the Mittagong Butterfly House.

Above: World-renowned cricketer, Sir Donald Bradman, played his early cricket in Bowral. The Bradman Oval is within walking distance of the station.

Left: Several trains a day connect Bowral with Sydney.

SYDNEY TO ARMIDALE

CITY TO THE HIGH COUNTRY

This is a beautifully scenic journey with a variety of landscapes from the picturesque Brisbane Waters, through agricultural landscapes to the rolling hills of the Great Dividing Range. From Sydney the train heads north towards Newcastle before travelling to the north-west through the Hunter Valley and across the Great Dividing Range to Armidale in the state's north-west.

Armidale is located on the Main North line (formerly the Great Northern Railway), which was once the main line to Brisbane, with a change of gauge at Wallangarra in southern Queensland. Although the Great Northern Railway was established in 1857, political indecision meant the rail to Armidale was only committed to in 1878 with the line finally reaching the city in 1883. In 1884, the line continued to Glen Innes but this section is now closed and the town serviced by coaches from Armidale.

THE TRAIN

The daily service from Sydney to Armidale operates as a five-car XPLORER train, which is divided at Werris Creek with the rear two cars being uncoupled for its westward journey to Moree. The other three carriages continue their journey northwards to their final destination of Armidale.

There are two classes and a buffet car but in the case of this train, these are duplicated before the train is divided for the Moree service.

THE JOURNEY

The train departs from Sydney Central Station at 9.29 a.m. and arrives in Armidale eight hours later at 5.35 p.m. The return service departs Armidale at 8.40 a.m. and arrives into Sydney Central at 4.38 p.m. The train stops at Strathfield, Hornsby, Gosford, Wyong, Fassifern, Broadmeadow, Maitland, Singleton, Muswellbrook, Aberdeen, Scone, Murrurundi, Willow Tree, Quirindi, Werris Creek, Tamworth, Kootingal, Walcha Road and Uralla before terminating at Armidale.

It passes through the forested extremities of suburban northern Sydney beyond Hornsby and crosses the Hawkesbury River at Brooklyn before gripping the tidal reaches of Brisbane Water. These waters are popular for fishing and watersports, while oyster leases can still be seen in the shallows though they are not as prolific as they once were. The train stops at Fassifern for the

connection to the branch line to the terminus of Toronto on the western shores of Lake Macquarie.

Broadmeadow is the stop for Newcastle passengers, the state's second largest city. Newcastle lies at the mouth of the Hunter River whose source is way up the Hunter Valley. Glimpses of the river can be seen at Hexham not long after the train departs Broadmeadow. Newcastle is the world's largest coal exporting port with much of this being railed from mines in the valley and beyond, so that what appears to be a conveyor belt of freight trains are common on the line from Broadmeadow through to Muswellbrook and Werris Creek.

Left: The Armidale train is divided at Werris Creek with two cars heading to Moree.

Below: The beautifully restored Armidale Railway Station is also home to a toy library.

TOY LIBRARY
6772 8838
CHILDREN'S
CENTRE
email: armidaletoylibrary@bigpond.com

Freight trains, operating as GRail, were once owned by mining giant Glencore but have been sold to Genesee & Wyoming Australia, a subsidiary of an American railway owner. GRail commenced operations in 2010 and is now Australia's third largest coal haulage business. While these mines generate billions of dollars in revenue they are not without controversy by being in conflict with the historical land uses, which are dairy farming and grape growing.

The Hunter Valley is renowned for its wines and there are scores of wineries located around Pokolbin, not far from Maitland and Singleton along the route. Well-respected Hunter Valley estates include Lindemans, McWilliam's, Wyndham Estate, Rosemount Estate, Rothbury, McGuigan and Tyrrell's. Varieties that thrive here include Semillon and Shiraz with aged Semillons considered some of the world's best. Wines from Glandore Estate in the Hunter Valley are served in New South Wales buffet cars. The train also passes close to wineries in the Upper Hunter Valley with Singleton and Muswellbrook being the best stations from which to access these.

Australia's horse capital is situated at Scone further northwards. Scone is famous for its expansive thoroughbred horse studs as well as for being an access point for the World Heritage-listed Barrington Tops National Park.

The train climbs slowly up over the Great Dividing Range and only stops at Murrurundi and Willow Tree upon request.

The journey is broken at Werris Creek, some 5.5 hours into the trip as the five-car train is divided and the back two cars are uncoupled to form the Werris Creek to Moree service. This train continues on to Moree via Gunnedah, Boggabri and Bellata before pulling into Moree at 6 p.m. This uncoupling takes ten minutes, maybe longer should one of the trains be late, but the good news is that time can be spent productively in the Australian Railway Monument and Rail Journeys Museum housed in the station's former refreshment room. Werris Creek has played a role in New

South Wales's rail history way beyond its small size. The historic Werris Creek Rail Depot and Junction was, during its heyday, the heart of 'the town that never slept'. Werris Creek became the main railway centre in northern New South Wales employing some 750 staff. Prior to electricity, gas was vital to strategic stations and Werris Creek was one of five stations in the state to have its own gas works. The others were Newcastle, Macdonaldtown, Bathurst and Junee. It thrived during the steam era from the 1870s to the 1960s and the museum, staffed by volunteers, has a superb collection of rail memorabilia.

After Werris Creek, the Armidale service operates as a three-car train inclusive of a buffet car. Thirty minutes later it pulls into Tamworth which is known throughout Australia as its country music capital with the annual Tamworth Country Music Festival in January the time when local and international singers, performers and audiences gather. Places to visit include the Golden Guitar, Hands of Fame Corner Store and the Country Music Roll of Renown. A coach service operates from here to Inverell.

After Kootingal the train starts to slowly climb on its circuitous route up through the range. It stops at Walcha Road, which appears to be in the middle of nowhere but there is a van service to Walcha some 20 minutes away.

Uralla with its heritage streetscape and historic buildings is the next town. The train terminates at the Armidale Railway Station, which has a heritage exterior but a functional and contemporary interior.

It is worth visiting the Armidale Bicentennial Railway Museum adjacent to the station. Winters in parts of Australia can get quite cold especially in the New England high country. Prior to the introduction of train gas heaters in the 1980s, foot warmers were used. Outside the museum visitors can admire a coal-fired boiler where footwarmers of old were pre-heated for long distance night trains. These foot warmers were metal boxes the size of a small suitcase filled with sodium silicate, a heat-retaining chemical.

Cathedrals and grand churches such as Saints Mary and Joseph Cathedral (Catholic), St Peter's Cathedral (Anglican) and St Paul's (Presbyterian) grace the city centre and the Mall has many grand, old and meticulously restored, heritage buildings. A walk reveals old hotels, the Court House, Post Office, Town Hall, Literary Institute and Central Park.

Above: The train from Moree approaching Werris Creek Station where it is connected to the Armidale to Sydney service.

Opposite: A small railway museum adjoins Armidale Railway Station.

SYDNEY TO THE SOUTH COAST

FAR FROM THE CARES OF THE WORLD

Trains on the South Coast or Illawarra Line are operated by NSW Trainlink Intercity with services starting from Bondi Junction and travelling via platform 25 beneath Central Station as far south as Bomaderry, with coach connections to Nowra situated on the Shoalhaven River 20 km (12½ miles) inland from the sea. These twin towns service the regional dairy industry and are a transport hub for coaches to destinations such as Jervis Bay and Kangaroo Valley. Passengers are required to use an Opal Card on the journey that takes some three hours over a distance of 153 km (93 miles).

Bomaderry was connected to Sydney by rail in 1888 but the line didn't make it across the Shoalhaven River to Nowra as the bridge was only for motor vehicles. Extensive goods yards were built next to Bomaderry Station that are still in use.

There are also vintage trains operated by 3801 Limited that travel on selected Wednesdays, Thursdays and Sundays from Sydney Central to Wollongong, then ascend the Illawarra Escarpment from Unanderra to Robertson and on to Moss Vale. Fully restored 1930s and 1940s carriages (with windows that open) are hauled by vintage diesel locomotives. Trains depart in the morning and return to Sydney at dusk.

THE TRAIN

Four and eight-car OSCAR electric trains operate to Kiama, where there is a train change to a multiple-unit diesel railcar comprising several carriages. The diesel train waits on the adjoining platform and departs soon after the train from Sydney arrives. Seating on OSCAR carriages is spread over two levels with five seats across. All carriages are non-smoking and air-conditioned, and quiet carriages are available (first, fourth, fifth, and eighth cars) where passengers must minimize any noise. Wheelchair access is provided and some stations have elevators for passengers with limited mobility. Audio announcements and digital displays of upcoming stations are made.

THE JOURNEY

Since around 2011, just a few South Coast trains continue to operate from 'country' platforms at Sydney's Central Station, with most services now beginning from Bondi Junction, stopping at all stations to Redfern. Emerging from the underground

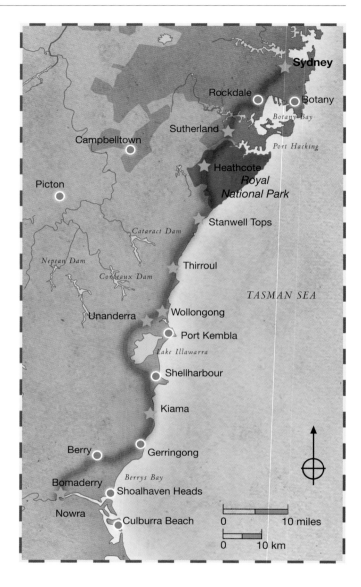

Eastern Suburbs Railway, the train then stops at Wolli Creek for Kingsford Smith International Airport. Trains cross a bridge over the Georges River and the landscape becomes greener as they proceed into Sutherland Shire. There is a stop at Sutherland for connecting trains to Cronulla.

At Heathcote passengers start to become acquainted with the delights of the Royal National Park on the eastern side of the line. Heathcote National Park is on the western side . By Helensburgh the land on both sides of the track is well-forested with sightings of

the original single line railway before the 1914 deviation, including abandoned cuttings, telegraph poles and old brick-lined tunnels. By Royal National Park both sides are surrounded by mature eucalypt forests. The park is popular with those wanting to explore the forests, trails, cliffs and beaches of Australia's oldest national park (and the world's second oldest) dating back to 1879.

A railway branch line once headed into the Royal National Park at Loftus, but while no longer serviced by the rail network, the Loftus Tramway Museum is just a short walk from Loftus station. This houses a selection of lovingly restored vintage trams including original 'Toastrack' and corridor Sydney Trams, linking with the Honeymoon Walking Trail that leads through the national park down to Audley. The museum also offers tram journeys towards Sutherland, with plans in place for the branch to be extended up to Sutherland along Rawson Parade, eventually terminating at the original tram stop opposite Boyles Hotel.

The first glimpse of the coastline and its famed beaches is as the train exits a tunnel before Stanwell Park, one hour after departure. Here, Bald Hill is an acclaimed hang-gliding site where novices can enjoy a tandem glide with an experienced instructor.

From here the train travels parallel to the coast through small towns, which have many weekender and holiday homes that are busiest in the summer months. Originally known as Robbinsville, Thirroul is one such settlement and it was here that English novelist D.H. Lawrence completed *Kangaroo* after a short sojourn in the town. The Thirroul Railway Institute Preservation Society operates from the railway station.

The skyline of Wollongong appears and from this city, trains stop at all stations to Kiama. There is a two-station branch line to Port Kembla, which is Wollongong's main industrial zone and home to the BlueScope Steel steelworks. Port Kembla is also a busy port for exporting coal from the southern and western parts of New South Wales with these trains being operated by Pacific National.

Another branch line from Unanderra heads inland to Robertson and Moss Vale (see page 66). Heritage trains called the Cockatoo Run operated by 3801 Limited travel on this line on select days.

Above: The train crosses the Georges River to the south of the Sydney Central Business District.

Above: Kiama Harbour is where fishing boats unload their catch and where fresh seafood is served in a few outlets.

Right: The train arrives into Kiama and crosses a bridge just before the station.

Opposite left: Sydney trains terminate at Kiama and there is a change of train on to Bomaderry.

Opposite right: The Kiama Blowhole is a popular tourist attraction on the South Coast and within walking distance of Kiama Railway Station.

Kiama Harbour with its small fishing fleet, seafood cafés and a beachfront lined with towering pines. The main street features grand Victorian buildings including the Westpac Bank, Council Chambers and the Post Office.

The diesel railcar from Kiama closely follows the coastline through lush farming land via Gerringong and Berry before reaching Bomaderry. Seats above the diesel engine are best avoided for the most comfortable ride.

Berry is a beautiful dairy-farming town with a farmers' market that is held on the first Sunday of every month. Bomaderry tends to be overshadowed by the larger town of Nowra although they are in effect, twin towns. Nowra entered Australian folklore when in 1861 and 1862 a locally trained horse named Archer won the first two Melbourne Cup races.

This coastal stretch is known for its racing tracks including Kembla Grange (horses), Dapto (dogs) and Albion Park (harness races). Illawarra Regional Airport is also located at Albion Park and is mostly used for small aircraft as well as being the home of the Historical Aircraft Restoration Society Aviation Museum. Located just a short walk from the station, the museum houses a Qantas 747-400 aircraft, the *City of Canberra*, which in 1989 flew from London to Sydney (a distance of 18,001 km/9,720 nautical miles) to break the record for the longest non-stop commercial flight of just under 20 hours. This record remains unbroken.

The best coastal views for the southward journey are on the train's left or eastern side although these seats are in the morning sun.

Open farmland extends either side of the line beyond Shellharbour Junction and for much of the remainder of the journey. Pockets of residential housing are replacing the dairy industry once synonymous with the area.

While Bombo is ideal for those seeking sand and surf, Kiama is the most popular coastal stop along the route and famous for its blowhole in the coastal rocks that lie within 500 m (547 yards) of the station. Other attractions include a rock pool for swimming,

SYDNEY TO DUBBO

SERVING THE CENTRAL WEST

The Dubbo train provides access to various tourist destinations along the way including the Blue Mountains, Bathurst, Orange and Wellington. The open plains Taronga Western Plains Zoo is one of the main reasons for travelling to Dubbo. This Central West XPT train covers a distance of some 462 km (287 miles).

Dubbo is on the Main Western Railway, which is an extension of the Sydney metropolitan network beyond the Blue Mountains where it continues westward to the main stops of Bathurst and Orange. At Orange, the Dubbo train branches off the line west to Broken Hill to head northwards passing through the main stations of Stuart Town, Wellington and Geurie before arriving in Dubbo.

The line reached Dubbo in 1881 which soon developed as a rail hub for onward trains that once operated to Coonamble, Narromine, Nyngan and Bourke.

Heavy 36, 38 and 60 class steam locomotives were used on the line to Dubbo and lighter locomotives continued beyond Dubbo. Overnight trains, such as the Dubbo Mail and Western Mail, once operated from Sydney but the service stopped in 1988.

The current daily train for Dubbo departs from Sydney Central at 7.18 a.m. and arrives at its destination some 6½ hours later at 1.45 p.m. At 2.15 p.m., the return train from Dubbo to Sydney Central departs and arrives into Sydney at 8.44 p.m.

Trains heading to Broken Hill in the far west of the state also operate on parts of the line between Sydney and Orange.

THE TRAIN

The Dubbo service operated by NSW TrainLink incorporates a five-carriage XPT train with diesel-electric XP locomotives at

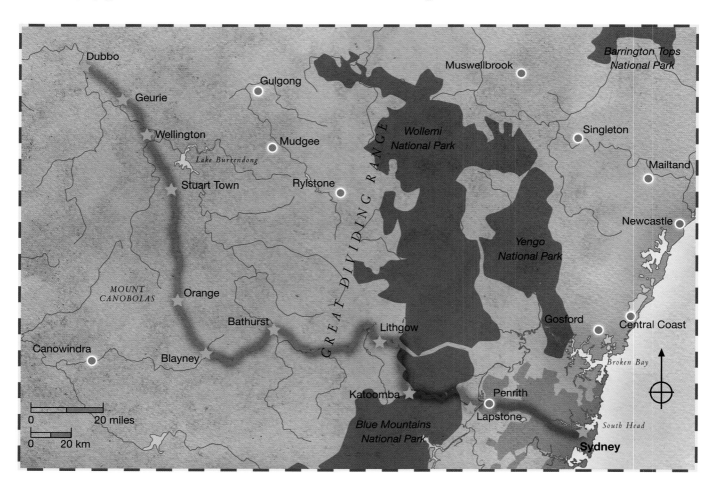

either end; one pulls and the other pushes. Trains on this service and other XPT routes can operate up to speeds of 120 km/h (75 mph). The name is an abbreviation for the Express Passenger Train that was introduced in New South Wales in 1982.

Passengers normally require a reserved seat before boarding the train but those who get on at more isolated stations get their tickets from the onboard train crew.

Passengers can travel in premium first class or economy class in comfortable seats and carriages with panoramic windows for admiring the ever-changing scenery. Two cars are for first class (one car has 56 seats), the buffet car has 21 first-class seats plus wheelchair access, while the two economy cars accommodate 68 passengers each. A further car for economy class takes 44 passengers and the rest of the space is a baggage compartment. At the end of each journey, train crews reverse the seats on a swivel so they always face the direction of travel.

Facilities are not available in the buffet car for consuming food or beverages, so passengers need to take their refreshments back to their reserved seats. The menu is the same as other long distance services operated by NSW Train Link (Sydney to Armidale and Sydney to Canberra, for example). Hot breakfasts are available

within minutes of departing Sydney Central while snacks, such as muffins, cake, apple pie, scones, and cheese and crackers, are available throughout the journey. Orders for hot meals are taken later in the journey. Hunter Valley wines, beer, cider, tea, coffee, juices and soft drinks are also available.

THE JOURNEY

The train heads through the Sydney suburbs to the Blue Mountains stopping at selected main stations. Beyond Katoomba and the Blue Mountains, it stops at Lithgow, Rydal, Tarana, Bathurst, Blayney, Orange, Stuart Town, Wellington and Geurie before arriving in Dubbo. The train only stops on request at the smaller stations, so passengers need to alert onboard train crew if they wish to get off at any of these.

Within 45 minutes of departure, the train crosses the bridge over the Nepean River and Sydney's urban sprawl starts to be replaced by forests. At Lapstone the train starts climbing up the escarpment of the Blue Mountains. Beyond the Blue Mountains, the train travels

Above: XPT trains at Sydney Central Station awaiting their morning departure to various locations including Dubbo.

down the western side of the escarpment at Lithgow and on to the more open plains and rolling hills of the Central West. It passes the Wallerawang Power Station, which is located immediately adjacent to a coal mine that provides the fuel to power the station.

While the train only stops at the small Terana Station on request, it travels slowly for ten minutes prior to arriving, which enables passengers to admire the agricultural land of rolling hills and lichen-encrusted boulders lining several meandering streams.

Just east of Bathurst, wheat fields dominate the landscape. Bathurst, adjacent to the Macquarie River, is 200 km (124 miles) west of Sydney and close to the site where gold was first discovered in Australia. While a cathedral city with impressive Catholic and Anglican structures, Bathurst is known to many for car racing on the Mount Panorama Circuit, south-west of the city centre.

Bathurst boomed when gold was discovered in the surrounding districts in the 1850s. It was also the home of Cobb & Co. horse-drawn coaches. One of the buffet cars on the XPT has a replica Cobb & Co. clock that was presented to the train service by Parkes Shire Council to mark the arrival of the inaugural Silver City XPLORER on June 23, 2002.

Orange has developed a reputation for being one of Australia's premium, cool-climate wine regions. The products are celebrated at the Orange Wine Festival held in mid to late October when the fine wines are accompanied by the best of the local produce prepared by acclaimed chefs. Orange F.O.O.D. Week in late March and early April is another event during which to enjoy the district's finest produce.

Wellington is famous for the caves just south of the town. Visitors can join guided tours of Gaden Cave, Cathedral Cave and a phosphate mine. Just beyond Wellington Railway Station, the train crosses a bridge over the Macquarie River named after a former New South Wales state governor.

Dubbo Railway Station on Talbragar Street is a beautiful old stone and brick building that retains much of its heritage both inside and out. Its interior has contemporary services but the old fireplaces are a reminder of a bygone era. The former two-storey stationmaster's residence in the adjacent carpark has been faithfully restored to its original grandeur. The predominant colour scheme of the railway station is cream and chocolate brown, as distinct from the other ochre and cream-coloured heritage stations along the way. Another grand building on the same street is the Dubbo Post Office.

Taronga Western Plains Zoo is located just out of the city centre on the Obley Road and its expansive open plains concept enables visitors to see local and exotic animals in a near-wild setting. Visitors can hire bicycles to move from one enclosure to another along a 6-km (3¾-mile) circuit. Cabins and campsites are available as is the Zoofari Lodge where guests can experience luxurious lodge accommodation close to the animals in a style similar to an African safari.

Above: Bathurst Railway Station.

Left: The Dubbo train at Dubbo Station.

Opposite: The stationmaster's cottage adjacent to the station has been meticulously restored.

AUSTRALIAN CAPITAL TERRITORY

INTRODUCTION

The Australian Capital Territory (ACT) includes the Australian capital city of Canberra as well as Parliament House, the home of the federal government. The site for the planned national capital was identified after the individual Australian states agreed to federate as the Commonwealth of Australia in 1901. Covering just 2,400 sq km (927 sq miles), the territory was identified as the new Australian capital in 1911. Canberra was chosen as a compromise between the two dominant state capitals of Sydney and Melbourne as it was approximately half-way between the two.

American architect Walter Burley Griffin and his wife were chosen from submissions from around the globe to develop a blueprint for a garden city of tree-lined avenues and numerous parklands. The vision was to transform pastoral land into an expansive parkland city around a lake.

While a rail route from what was then known as Eastlake (now Kingston and the only place now with any railway activity in the ACT) to the northern and eastern parts of Canberra was envisaged, it never materialized. However, the need for a rail link to Canberra was recognized early and in 1913 work started on the construction of an 8.5-km (5⅓-mile) branch line to Canberra from Queanbeyan located on the Goulburn to Bombala line in neighbouring New South Wales. Its construction was undertaken by the NSW Public Works Department for the Federal Government and in 1914, the first steam locomotive pulled into Canberra. These early trains only carried freight.

In 1917, Commonwealth Railways of Australia (later to be Australian National) was established to administer the Trans-Australia (SA to WA link), the Port Augusta (SA) to Darwin (NT) link and the Australian Capital Territory Railway. While owned and staffed by Commonwealth Railways, the Canberra service was operated by NSW Government Railways (later to be NSW State Rail Authority).

The first Canberra Railway Station opened in 1924 enabling passenger trains to operate on the line. In 1927 Canberra officially became the seat of the national parliament after relocating from its temporary home in Melbourne. This necessitated the upgrading of rail services to the capital with the introduction of both a night and a day train. A Canberra link was provided to the overnight Cooma Mail to Sydney, which was timed to meet the Melbourne sleeper train at Goulburn Junction. In 1936, the Federal City Express day train from Sydney was introduced to complement the evening service.

Over the years, upgraded services were introduced with air-conditioning and diesel-hauled locomotives being the main features. In 1955, multiple-unit diesel rail cars were introduced to what became known as the Canberra-Monaro Express.

The former wooden station was replaced by a brick one and the current Canberra Railway Station at Kingston was opened in 1966. In 1983, XPT services were introduced and in 1985, the operations of the station and rail link to Queanbeyan reverted to New South Wales. The Bombala to Cooma line was closed in 1986 and in 1988, the southern line from Canberra to Cooma train ceased operations. XPT trains from Sydney to Canberra were withdrawn in 1990 but in 1993, XPLORER trains were introduced and remain in service on the line.

LINKS TO THE PAST

While Griffin's rail plans didn't materialise, several small train lines were established within the ACT mainly to assist with the construction of public buildings. The first to open, albeit briefly, was a line that branched off the Queanbeyan to Canberra line and headed north across the Molonglo River to behind the current Parliament House terminating with a marshalling yard in Braddon. Work on the line commenced in 1920 and was completed a year later but within a few years, floodwaters washed away the legs of a trestle bridge across the Molonglo and the line never reopened.

In 1923, a line was constructed from the Yarralumla (or Commonwealth) Brickworks to the site of the Old Parliament House on King George Terrace in the Canberra suburb of Parkes. Bricks for Parliament House were transported along this line but once the building was completed, the track was removed for the opening ceremony, which was performed by the Duke and Duchess of York in 1927. This acted as Parliament House until the new Parliament House on Capital Hill behind the old building was opened in 1988. Old Parliament House now houses the Museum of Democracy.

BACK TO THE FUTURE

These days, politicians, public servants and the other residents of Canberra need to move about quickly, so Canberra Airport is now much busier than Kingston Railway Station. There have been discussions about constructing a Canberra light rail network but there are still no definite plans. A possible train link from Yass Junction to Canberra has been surveyed but nothing has come from this assessment.

Apart from the direct rail link to Sydney, the other options for rail passengers are coach connections to the New South Wales destinations of Yass Junction, Cootamundra, Bombala and Eden, while Victoria's V/Line provides a Canberra to Bairnsdale service with connections on to Melbourne.

Canberra Railway Museum is located within eyesight of the Canberra Railway Station on Cunningham Street, Kingston, but it is currently not operational.

Above: The Australian Parliament House building, opened in Canberra in 1988, is a taxi ride away from Canberra Railway Station located in Kingston.

CANBERRA TO SYDNEY

CAPITAL EXPLORER

Despite Canberra being situated between Sydney and Melbourne, it is not located on the train line between the two but it is possible for passengers travelling between Australia's two largest cities to alight at Yass Junction and take a coach to Canberra. An XPLORER train service from Canberra to Sydney is the principal rail connection between the capital and Australia's largest city.

Canberra Railway Station is in suburban Kingston to the south-east of Lake Burley Griffin and to the east of Capital Hill, where the flagpole on top of Parliament House towers over the Australian capital. Function rather than appearance is important at Canberra Station which is only staffed prior to trains departing

and arriving. The station has a modern waiting room and a ticket counter. The station adjoins the Canberra Railway Museum but the museum is currently closed and its future is uncertain. One of its prized steam locomotives is an AD60 class Beyer-Garratt locomotive weighing 265 tonnes (282 tons).

Canberra is an expansive garden city with large green areas and numerous traffic roundabouts. One of the best and most popular ways to take in the vastness of Canberra is to soar over it in a hot-air balloon. While weather dependent, there are flights on most days at sunrise when the air is the most stable and calm. Flights are celebrated with a traditional Champagne toast at the end of the trip.

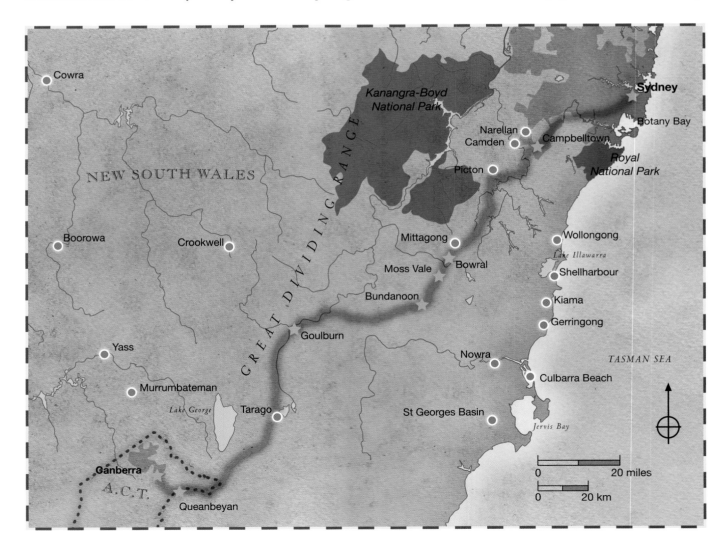

Left: The train arriving from Sydney into Kingston Station in Canberra.

Below: The brick rail viaduct (centre of photo) spans Mulwaree Ponds in Goulburn and is the longest viaduct on the Main Southern Railway Line with 13 arches.

Snow on a few days of winter is not unusual in Canberra but for skiing and other snow sports, Canberra residents drive a few hours south to the Snowy Mountains and Australia's highest peak of Mount Kosciuszko at 2,228 m (7,310 ft). The ski fields and alpine meadows of Thredbo, Perisher Valley and Charlotte Pass are well-equipped to cater to skiers during the winter months as well as a range of summertime activities, such as hiking, camping and horseback riding.

THE TRAIN

Facilities exist on the three-car XPLORER service for wheelchair access via portable ramps. Car A incorporates a buffet counter and premium-class seating for approximately 30 passengers. The two other carriages are for economy-class passengers with seating for 67 in each car. The windows extend over two seats to provide excellent viewing of the passing countryside. Passengers can check in luggage at Canberra and collect it from the luggage compartment at the front of the train at their destination.

THE JOURNEY

Trains depart from Sydney Central for Canberra at 7.04 a.m. (6.57 a.m. at the weekend), 12.08 p.m. and 6.12 p.m. Trains for Sydney Central depart Canberra at 6.50 a.m., 11.53 p.m. (11.40 a.m. at weekends) and 5.25 p.m. (5.20 p.m. at weekends).

Some passengers joining the train in Canberra arrive at Canberra Station via coaches operated by NSW TrainLink. These services operate from Bombala, Eden, Yass Junction and Cootamundra.

Within seconds of departing Canberra the train is travelling through grazing land and tree-lined streams. Not long after, the train passes into New South Wales without any indication of a border crossing and arrives in the beautiful painted brick station at Queanbeyan on the banks of the Molonglo River. The railway first arrived in Queanbeyan in 1887 which soon became an important junction on the lines to Canberra and also Bombala in southern New South Wales.

Bungendore on the Kings Highway is an historic village classified by the National Trust. Located in the Molonglo Valley near

Lake George, its many restored buildings are much visited. Tarago is bypassed if there are no passengers getting on or off. The train arrives into Goulburn 90 minutes after leaving Canberra. This is a regional service centre for the rich pastoral farmlands in the Southern Tablelands including the Goulburn Plains and the high country around Crookwell to the north-west. It was proclaimed as Australia's first inland city in 1863 and the railway arrived soon after in 1869. Branch lines were constructed not long afterwards to Cooma, Nimmitabel and Bombala in the south, Crookwell (north-west) and Taralga (north). The Goulburn Court House built in 1887 is considered one of the finest country courthouses in the state. In stark contrast is the Big Merino, a popular rest stop for motorists travelling along the Hume Highway from Sydney to Melbourne.

The first stop in the Southern Highlands is Bundanoon two hours after departing the national capital. Like other towns and villages of the Southern Highlands, Bundanoon blossomed with the arrival of the railway in 1868. The railway station here was originally called Jordan's Crossing, then Jordan's Siding before being named Bundanoon in 1881.

Bundanoon, like the Blue Mountains, became accessible to city residents who travelled here by train to admire the scenery and enjoy the healthy air. This was an era when a train journey of a few hours from the city was considered a big adventure. Nearby Morton National Park was, and still is, a popular place for walking, picnicking and sightseeing. In April each year, Brigadoon is celebrated in the town and is one of the largest highland gatherings in the southern hemisphere.

Other stops in the Southern Highlands are made at Moss Vale, Bowral (see page 66) and Mittagong. Three and half hours into the trip, the train has reached Campbelltown on the outskirts of Sydney and just before 4 p.m., the train pulls into its terminus at Sydney Central Railway Station.

Opposite: Coaches also connect to Yass Junction for trains to Melbourne and Sydney.

Below: Visitors to Canberra's Cockington Green Gardens can admire a fascinating display of miniature buildings and a model railway set in beautiful gardens.

QUEENSLAND

INTRODUCTION

Australia's second largest state covers 1.73 million sq km (666,876 sq miles) or 22.5 per cent of the country. While 4.75 million people live in what is known as the 'Sunshine State', the population is mostly concentrated in the south-east and along the coast. Agriculture and mining have always been important to the state and the railways have served a vital function for many of Queensland's remote inland communities.

Like most other Australian states, a penal colony was established in Queensland in 1824 with the original settlement relocating in 1825 to where the capital Brisbane now stands. Queensland became a separate colony from neighbouring New South Wales in 1859.

This huge but sparsely settled colony needed to export its commodities to the world and its first railway opened in 1865. This line ran from Ipswich to Bigge's Camp (renamed as Grandchester) and it was the first narrow gauge (1,067 mm/3 foot 6 inch) mainline railway in the world. Narrow gauge was a cheaper option than wide gauge but the decision was controversial at the time.

This line was extended to Toowoomba and reached Dalby by 1868. However, Brisbane was not connected by rail until 1875 and then the line only ran to Indooroopilly with freight and passengers transferred across the Brisbane River initially by ferry until the Albert Bridge was built.

SERVING THE STATE

It was envisaged that a railway network would further develop the colony especially as minerals such as gold became unearthed during the various gold rushes. Those who supported an expansion to the railway network inland were encouraged by the mostly flat terrain that made track construction easy. A policy to develop a decentralized network centred on several coastal ports was adopted to service mining and pastoral interests in the interior.

Substantial funds were injected into railway infrastructure especially in the 1880s which witnessed a railway boom. It wasn't only miners who garnered the attention of the politicians as graziers and pastoralists were just as vocal with their demands to be serviced by efficient rail connections. Railway lines went west from Rockhampton to Barcaldine in 1886, then to Charleville (1888) and through to Longreach (1892). Moving sheep around

the state, especially during periods of drought, was important and the railway served this function. At its peak in 1932, there were 10,500 km (6,524 miles) of railway track in the state.

Over time, transporting minerals to market became increasingly important and by 2010 the Queensland Government decided to split its railway system, retaining control of the Government-owned passenger operator Queensland Railway while selling off the freight operator QR National (now Aurizon). Aurizon is one of Australia's largest rail freight operators contolling one of the world's largest coal rail networks comprising 50 mines and three exporting ports.

A HARSH LANDSCAPE

While many choose to live in Queensland because of the favourable climate, climatic extremes can wreak havoc with cyclones, floods and high temperatures impacting on the rail network. Much of inland Queensland is hot and dry for most of the year, but monsoonal rains can turn the parched landscape into raging torrents in hours, as many stranded passengers have discovered. Australia's highest temperature ever recorded was in Cloncurry in 1889 at 53.1°C/127.5°F.

Several iconic trains are operated by Queensland Rail in the state's often harsh climate. These include the *Spirit of Queensland* (Brisbane to Cairns), the *Spirit of the Outback* (Brisbane to Longreach), the Tilt Train (Brisbane to Rockhampton), the *Westlander* (Brisbane to Charleville), *The Inlander* (Townsville to Mount Isa), *The Gulflander* (Normanton to Croydon) and the Kuranda Scenic Railway (Cairns to Kuranda).

A privately-managed rail touring service called *Savannahlander* operates a weekly service from Cairns to Forsayth using a vintage two-car railmotor on a journey that lasts several days and involves overnight stops in hotels along the way.

Opposite: The *Spirit of Queensland* passes the Glass House Mountains in the Sunshine Coast hinterland.

THE *SPIRIT OF QUEENSLAND*: BRISBANE TO CAIRNS

CITY TO THE REEF

At 3.45 p.m. the shrill of the conductor's whistle captures the attention of passengers already on board the *Spirit of Queensland* as well as school children returning home and early commuters lining Brisbane's main railway station.

The *Spirit of Queensland* departs from platform 10 of Brisbane's Roma Street Station daily except for Thursdays and Sundays to Cairns, 1,681 km (1,045 miles) away in Tropical North Queensland. It arrives into Cairns Station on the day after departing Brisbane at 4.05 p.m. This journey in spacious black leather seats redefines the modern rail travel experience, and provides a convenient and comfortable way to take in the dynamic capital city of Queensland as well as to access some of Queensland's amazing coastal destinations while also offering a gateway to several iconic inland rail journeys. Return journeys from Cairns depart daily except for Tuesdays and Saturdays at 9 a.m. and arrive into Brisbane at 9.20 a.m. the next day.

A growth in tourism in Cairns and its hinterland was anticipated with the completion of the railway line between Brisbane and Cairns in 1924. This line also enabled travellers to journey all the way from Cairns on Australia's East Coast to Perth located on the West Coast with a few changes of trains along the way. The service from Cairns to Townsville was initially twice weekly with a connection on the Up Mail from Townsville to Brisbane. The journey from Brisbane to Cairns took 40 hours with an overnight stay in Townsville on the way.

THE TRAIN

Various trains operated on sections of the line including the *Townsville Mail* and the *Sunshine Express*. In 1953, the Brisbane to Cairns service became known as *The Sunlander*, replacing the *Sunshine Express*. This train operated for 61 years before the *Spirit of Queensland* introduced its current version of luxurious train travel.

There are now two trains operating on sections of this line – the *Spirit of Queensland* to Cairns and what are called Tilt Trains, which commenced operations in 1998 along the northern line, between Brisbane and Rockhampton. Tilt Trains are so called because they can tilt five degrees in each direction, passenger trains can operate at speeds of up to 160 km/h (99 mph). At the time of their introduction, these new electric trains were the fastest narrow-gauge trains in the world cutting the travelling time by 33 per cent.

A consortium that included Hitachi (Japan), Evans Deakin (Australia) and Walkers (Australia) supplied sets of stainless-steel carriages, the diesel-electric locomotives were supplied by Goninans (Australia). *Spirit of Queensland* trains are capable of carrying 310 passengers (30 in RailBed and 280 in Premium Economy) while Tilt Trains have 30 premium and 260 economy seats. Tilt Trains have operated on the Cairns service since 2003.

Passengers travelling in premium or RailBed class enjoy facilities equivalent to business-class travel on leading global airlines with an Australian first; the revolutionary RailBed which was introduced on the service in 2013. In the early evening, the spacious day seat is converted by the train crew to a lengthy, lie-flat bed with a mattress topper and linen. Passengers can adjust the seat themselves during the day to a near flatbed with a seat recline of 35 degrees.

A toiletries amenities kit is provided as are towels for a refreshing shower in very spacious cubicles designed for wheelchair access. Toilets are available in the same space as well as in dedicated places in other parts of the train.

Left: The *Spirit of Queensland* about to depart Brisbane's Roma Street Station.

RailBed seating is three seats across; a double and a single either side of the aisle. The inside window seat is marginally bigger than the aisle seat.

A 47-cm (18½-inch) television screen is housed in the back of the seat in front. There is a magazine rack attached to a moveable section of the seat in front that pulls down in the evening to form the footrest for the bed. An audio commentary of the route is available and announcements are made prior to the train arriving in stations where it stops.

RailBed customers also enjoy all-inclusive meals served directly to their seat. Meals take a paddock-to-plate approach to showcase some of Queensland's wonderful produce. A typical three-course dinner could include a tomato basil and boccocini salad, beef striploin with garlic mushrooms, truffle mash and green beans, and raspberry financier with clotted cream; all accompanied by a complimentary juice, beer or wine. A continental or full hot breakfast is served. Lunch is a more modest, two-course meal such as smoked chicken plus chocolate cheesecake served with a complimentary beverage. There is also a Club Car where snacks and beverages are available outside of meal times. Queensland wines sourced from Mount Cotton and the Granite Belt are proudly served along with Queensland's popular lager beer, XXXX and its favourite rum – Bundaberg.

Premium Economy seats are also available and offer comfortable seating, generous legroom and a state-of-the-art, 23-cm (9-in) personal entertainment system. Leather seats recline at 30 degrees, there is a power point, overhead lockers and a reading light.

Tilt Trains also operate on parts of this line from Brisbane to Rockhampton (639 km/397 miles). This journey takes 7.5 hours with departures from Brisbane on Tuesday, Friday and Sunday and from Rockhampton on Monday, Thursday and Saturday. The refurbished *City of Maryborough* Tilt Train has features such as a licensed Galley Car and complimentary wi-fi.

THE JOURNEY

There's no escaping the 'tyranny of distance' in Australia with the journey from Brisbane to Cairns taking 24 hours. Features of the tropical weather along the journey are high humidity and high temperatures.

Major towns from south to north include Gympie, Maryborough (with coach connection to Hervey Bay), Bundaberg, Gladstone, Rockhampton (coach to Yeppoon), Mackay, Proserpine (coach to Airlie Beach), Bowen, Townsville, Ingham, Tully and Innisfail.

Several iconic Queensland rail journeys head west from the main north-south line to provide access to the state's interior. From Brisbane, the *Westlander* train heads westward to Charleville and further onwards to Quilpie and Cunnamulla by coach. Passengers can also depart Brisbane on the *Spirit of the Outback* (see page 94), which travels north to Rockhampton, then westward to Longreach. Townsville is the departure station for the *Inlander* to Mount Isa (see page 96) and Cairns is the departure station for the *Savannahlander*, which heads south-west over the Atherton Tablelands to Forsayth.

While many travellers on the *Spirit of Queensland* continue all the way to Cairns, others use the train as a means of exploring coastal Queensland by getting off at various stations and rejoining the train later. Overseas travellers who find this appealing should consider purchasing a Queensland Explorer Pass which enables unlimited travel in economy class on most trains (and connecting coach services) operated in the state (however, the Kuranda Scenic Railway is not included) for a period of one or two months.

Even before the train arrives into Caboolture at the outer extremity of the Brisbane urban area, a rural landscape has already unfolded with farming land interspersed with suburban Brisbane.

The train passes the distinctive Glass House Mountains on the left-hand side before arriving in Nambour, which is the gateway for the Sunshine Coast, Noosa Heads and sub-tropical hinterland townships such as Eumundi and Montville. The train arrives in the late afternoon to enable those who choose to alight, to travel to their accommodation in a resort region that is less developed than the Gold Coast. The Sunshine Coast offers a delightful combination of sun-drenched beaches, cities and a rural hinterland with the main coastal resort towns from the south to the north being Caloundra, Mooloolaba, Maroochydore, Coolum and Noosa.

Nambour was once home to the passenger and sugar-cane railway known as the Nambour to Coolum Tramline. Sugar cane is grown in many parts of northern Queensland with old railway lines clearly visible near sections of the main line. The tramline in Nambour was once part of the Moreton Central Sugar Mill Cane Tramway that operated from around 1897 to 2001 with parts of the line still visible in several Nambour streets. Such tramways and rail lines comprised wagons initially hauled by steam locomotives and served an important role in transporting the harvested cane to the sugar mills. Many had a two foot (600 mm) gauge to minimize costs.

Apart from lazing on near-deserted beaches, other attractions on the Sunshine Coast include Australia Zoo (the home of the late 'crocodile hunter' Steve Irwin), Buderim Ginger, camel riding along the beach and the Eumundi Markets (Wednesdays and Saturdays). Noosa is a chic beachside resort town that especially appeals to Australians living in southern states who travel here in the winter to enjoy the year-round sunshine and upmarket lifestyle.

Passengers can alight at Maryborough (Maryborough West Station) with transfers to Hervey Bay at dusk to explore the World Heritage-listed Fraser Island a few kilometres offshore, whose pristine beauty includes freshwater lakes. One of the biggest employers in Maryborough is Downer Rail (formerly Walkers), which was responsible for building much of the rolling stock and locomotives for Queensland Rail.

The train arrives into Bundaberg in the dark and passengers wishing to explore the city will have to spend the night here. At Mon Repos near Bundaberg, turtles can be seen between October and April. The city is famous for the Bundaberg Distilling Company where it's possible to taste the iconic Bundaberg Rum.

Right: Train staff convert day seats for RailBed passengers into very comfortable beds in the evening.

Opposite: Sugar cane is one of the main crops passengers can see from the train window with Queensland providing 95 per cent of Australia's total production.

The Great Barrier Reef officially starts just north of Bundaberg but there are many places from here northwards for accessing the coral and associated tropical islands. The reef is the world's largest expanse of coral (over 2,300 km/1,429 miles long), the largest structure built by living organisms, and covers an area of 344,400 sq km (132,980 sq miles). It is larger then the combined areas of the United Kingdom, Holland and Switzerland or half the size of Texas.

Several islands along the reef from south to north, such as Great Keppel, Brampton, the Whitsundays (Hamilton and Hayman Islands), Magnetic, Hinchinbrook, Dunk, Fitzroy, Green and Lizard Islands, are home to resorts that especially cater to global holidaymakers.

By now, the train is well and truly travelling in the dark and passing through Gladstone and Rockhampton (for Yeppoon), then crossing the Tropic of Capricorn at 23°S. The train arrives in Rockhampton just before midnight. Some passengers alight here and spend time in the city before rejoining the *Spirit of Queensland* the next day or taking the *Spirit of the Outback*, which arrives very early in the morning and heads west to Longreach.

The arrival time into Proserpine at sunrise is a little more civilized. This is the station for passengers planning to travel via coach to Airlie Beach and then by boat to the islands in the Whitsundays.

Various stops are made between Townsville and Cairns with Tully being especially popular amongst adventurous young travellers who stop here to white-water raft on wild rivers flowing through the Tully Gorge National Park or to kayak on Bulban Creek.

Cairns is a busy arrival gateway for international flights and one of the main departure ports for trips to the Great Barrier Reef. It is especially popular with global backpackers who travel here to explore the Great Barrier Reef and its laid-back holiday lifestyle. North of Cairns, the Great Barrier Reef meets the lush, World Heritage-listed, tropical rainforests along the coastline. These are two of the most species-abundant ecosystems on Earth.

From Cairns, the train up the escarpment to Kuranda is considered one of Australia's greatest tourist train journeys (see page 100).

Cooktown to the north of Cairns is a remote outpost of civilization along the Tropical North Queensland coast while destinations such Port Douglas, Mossman, Palm Cove and the Daintree are popular tourists destinations also to the north of Cairns.

BRISBANE TO THE GOLD COAST

SURFERS' PARADISE ON A GOLD COAST

Queensland's Gold Coast encapsulates Australia's international image as a sun-drenched country where most people swim out from golden sandy beaches. The Gold Coast is arguably Australia's number one beachside holiday destination, which offers not only surf, sun and sand but also rainforests in its hinterland, a vibrant lifestyle and numerous theme parks. Many international visitors arrive directly into either the Gold Coast Airport or Brisbane International Airport.

Trains from Brisbane to Beenleigh first operated in 1885 with the line extended southward to Southport in 1889. Stanley Street in South Brisbane was the original city terminus for the line. The Beenleigh to Southport line closed in 1964 and the line from Brisbane to Beenleigh was electrified in 1982. Construction of the newly-aligned Gold Coast line commenced in 1996 and reached the Varsity Lakes terminus in 2009.

Trains operating from Brisbane Airport, travel via Brisbane's Roma Street Station before heading south to Varsity Lakes, inland from the Gold Coast's main beaches. Bus services are timed to meet the trains with most then heading to the coastal transport hub of Broadbeach South. Trams on the G:line head north from Broadbeach South and connect to many coastal attractions and beaches. Therefore, it's possible to travel from Brisbane Airport to the Gold Coast using trains, buses and trams within this network.

KDR Gold Coast is the operator and maintainer of the Gold Coast's tram system while McConnell and Bombardier jointly delivered the system's design and construction. Services began in mid-2014 and will serve a valuable transportation function during the Commonwealth Games to be staged on the Gold Coast in April 2018.

Currumbin Wildlife Sanctuary offers a completely different experience, enabling visitors to get close to some of Australia's unique wildlife in a natural forest setting situated between Currumbin Creek and the ocean.

The mountainous hinterland offers another unique setting with many parts blanketed in sub-tropical rainforest interspersed with pockets of farming and residential land.

Northern New South Wales isn't that far from Gold Coast Airport with coastal towns such as Byron Bay and attractions like the Tropical Fruit World, within an hour's drive.

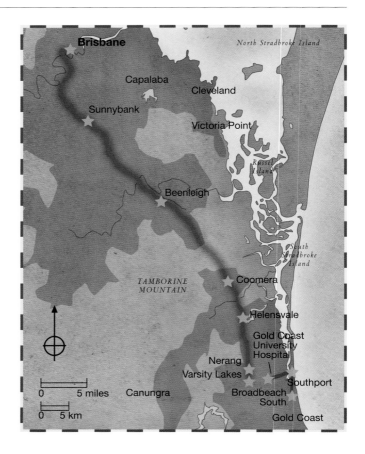

THE TRAIN

TRANSLink is responsible for operating the train service between Brisbane and the Gold Coast. It is a division of the Queensland Department of Transport and Main Roads and provides public transport in various parts of the state including the south-east between Gympie in the north and Coolangatta in the south. It does this in partnership with Queensland Rail, which provides services on various lines with its rolling stock of electric multiple-unit trains.

Meanwhile, trams on the G:link Gold Coast service are similar to those used in some other Australia cities, such as those on the Adelaide to Glenelg service (see page 34).

THE JOURNEY

Trains start from the Brisbane Domestic Airport, then four minutes later arrive at the International Terminal. The next stop is Brisbane

Roma Street Station 28 minutes later and the train arrives at the Varsity Lakes terminus 80 minutes after departure. Trains operate from 5 a.m. with the final departure at 10 p.m. These trains don't

Above: G:link trams connect Gold Coast destinations from Gold Coast University Hospital southwards to Broadbeach South.

Top: The train passes through Robina adjacent to the CBus Super Stadium which is home to the Titans rugby league team and was the venue for the rugby sevens during the Commonwealth Games.

stop at all stations but once at Beenleigh on the Gold Coast, they stop at every station to Varsity Lakes.

While there are no seamless connections via the train to the theme parks, Coomera Station is best for Dreamworld and Helensvale for Warner Bros. Movie World, Wet 'N' Wild and the Australian Outback Spectacular.

Bus services provide a valuable link between trains from Brisbane and G:link trams. This tram or light rail system of 16 stations offers an excellent way to explore several destinations. Trams starts from Broadbeach South hub in the front of Pacific Fair, Queensland's largest mall and take 33 minutes to reach the northern terminus of University Hospital. The tram travels down the centre of the road for much of the journey.

G:link trams have modern interiors with comfortable seating, space to store surfboards and wheelchair access with dedicated wheelchair areas inside. Digital and audio information announces the next stop.

Some of the places of interest and relevant stations along the route include Conrad Jupiters and the Convention Centre (Broadbeach North), Q1 and SkyPoint Observation Deck (Surfers Paradise), shopping, dining and clubs (Cavill Avenue), Chinatown (Southport), Griffith University (Griffith University) and Gold Coast Hospital (University Hospital).

THE *SPIRIT OF THE OUTBACK*: BRISBANE TO LONGREACH

ROCKHAMPTON TO LONGREACH

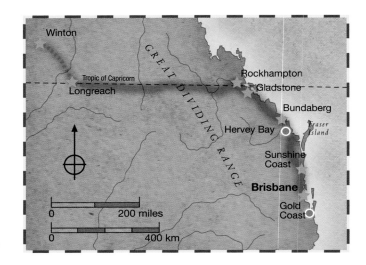

Many visitors to Australia are attracted to the vast open spaces and the ever-changing colours of Outback Australia. The *Spirit of the Outback* enables them to experience the scenery in air-conditioned comfort and to access Queensland destinations such as Rockhampton on the way. This journey of approximately 25 hours covers 1,325 km (823 miles) travelling through parts of coastal Queensland and the state's expansive interior.

The train operated by Queensland Rail was established when two pre-existing services were combined in 1993. From 1970 to 1993, *The Capricornian* passenger train serviced the North Coast line from Brisbane to Rockhampton, while *The Midlander* operated between 1954 and 1993 on the Central West line from Rockhampton to Winton. Both services were combined in 1993 as the *Spirit of the Outback*. When the first railway arrived in 1892 it was a vital link for inland settlers and for exporting rural produce, but now it's tourism that bolsters the region's economy.

THE TRAIN

Passengers can travel in first-class luxury or in the spacious surrounds of economy class. First-class travellers can enjoy all-inclusive meals freshly prepared in the Tuckerbox Dining Car and relax in the Shearers Rest Lounge. Takeaway meals and beverages are available to other passengers from the Shearers Rest Servery.

Premium passengers travel in a private compartment that converts to a comfortable bed for a restful night's sleep. Sleeping compartments are available as singles or doubles with both set-ups offering wardrobes, power points, bedding and towels. A table is included in double compartments and in the evening, the top bunk is folded down from the wall by the crew. Passengers also have access to complimentary tablets for viewing various entertainment channels. Drinking fountains plus shower and toilet facilities are provided at the end of each sleeping and seating carriage.

THE JOURNEY

Trains depart from Brisbane's Roma Street Station twice a week on Tuesday (6.10 p.m.) and Saturday (1.55 p.m.), arriving into Longreach 25 hours later (Wednesday at 7.20 p.m. and Sunday at 3.40 p.m.). Return trains depart Longreach on Monday and Thursday at the same time of 10 a.m. and arrive in Brisbane

on Tuesday and Friday at 11.55 a.m. With two choices on the journey to Longreach, passengers need to decide which parts of the route they want to see in daylight as the initial section on Tuesday is mostly traversed in the dark while on Saturday, it's possible to view coastal stretches but then parts of the inland are missed.

Most passengers take the full journey from Brisbane to Longreach and wake up on the second day to the colourful outback near Emerald. While it's possible to break the journey in Rockhampton, both trains travelling to and returning from Longreach arrive into Rockhampton city centre in the middle of the night. An alternative is to use the Tilt Train or *Spirit of Queensland* (see page 88), then join the *Spirit of the Outback* in Rockhampton.

After a journey of some 700 km (430 miles) from the coast at Rockhampton, the train arrives into Longreach in the early evening (Wednesday) or late afternoon (Sunday). Longreach located on the Tropic of Capricorn in the state's Central West offers tourism facilities way beyond what most would expect from a town of just over 3,000 residents. It is located at the junction of a major stock route and the banks of the Thomson River and has witnessed millions of livestock and thousands of stockmen passing through. Visitors come to enjoy the Stockman's Hall of Fame, opened in 1988, which pays tribute to Outback pioneers, and is dedicated to the Aboriginal community and stockmen of the Outback.

Longreach is also where the Queensland and Northern Territory Aerial Services Ltd. (Qantas), Australia's most recognized domestic and international airline, was established in 1920. The airline's

original hangar is retained at the airport and the Qantas Founders Outback Museum, housing a Consolidated PBY Catalina Flying Boat, Douglas DC-3, decommissioned Boeing 747-200 and the airline's first jet aircraft, a Boeing 707, are displayed here.

There is no longer a rail service to Winton but RailBus coaches now operate between Longreach and Winton - a two-hour drive (177 km / 110 miles) from Longreach. A train line from Hughenden (see The *Inlander* page 96) reached Winton in 1899 and the Central Western line arrived in Winton in 1928. Coach departures and arrivals to and from Winton are timed to provide a seamless service between the two destinations.

Located on the banks of the Western River, Winton too is one of the first homes for Qantas. Its other link to aviation history is that in June 1942 during the Second World War, a United States congressman recovered in Winton's North Gregory Hotel after surviving a plane crash south-west of the town. That congress-man just happened to be Lyndon B. Johnson who later became the President of the United States.

Winton has etched itself into Australian folk history due to the fact that Australia's alternative national anthem, *Waltzing Matilda* is based on a poem written by Banjo Paterson, penned when he visited Dagworth Station near Winton in 1895.

Above: Visit the Qantas Founders Outback Museum in Longreach.

Opposite: The train passes through a variety of landscapes from forested hills to the semi-desert of the Outback.

THE INLANDER: TOWNSVILLE TO MOUNT ISA

TROPICAL COAST TO THE OUTBACK

Townsville Railway Station is nearly deserted as *The Inlander* train departs after midday for the 21-hour, 977-km (607-mile) journey westwards. Opened in 2003, the station on the city's outskirts is functional but lacks the heritage of the former Townsville Railway Station. Train buffs should visit the old station to admire the grand three-storey brick and stone structure dating back to 1913 and learn about its history as documented by platform interpretation displays.

Townsville is a port for exporting minerals rail-freighted from Mount Isa's mines and others in the region. The city is also the gateway to Magnetic Island and its attractive beaches just a short boat trip away.

Train services to and from Mount Isa opened in April 1929 with the completion of the line from Duchess. However, there were earlier services on various sections including the Townsville Railway and the service to Charters Towers in 1882. The line reached Hughenden in 1887, Richmond in 1904, and Julia Creek and Cloncurry in 1908. It wasn't until 1953 that the first air-conditioned passenger train, *The Inlander* began operations. A branch freight line to Phosphate Hill opened in 1972.

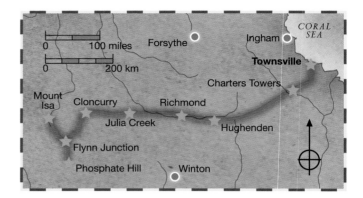

THE TRAIN

There are three carriages behind the Clyde diesel electric loco-motive; one is a combined lounge/staff car and the other two are sitting cars of slightly different configuration. Car A has 36 seats of a double and a single either side of the aisle while Car B has four seats across; two each on either side of the aisle. Car A is the favoured car because there is more space and this is where passengers are normally seated, while Car B offers more privacy. One

Right: A whistle blast and *The Inlander* is on its long journey to Mount Isa.

Opposite: While trains no longer operate from the original Townsville Railway Station, it is well worth visiting to get a sense of the city's rail history.

of the best views from the train for the scenery and photography is from the rear of the last carriage, which has a viewing window.

All cars are air conditioned, without which the atmosphere would be stifling especially near Mount Isa where the summer mercury often exceeds 40°C (104°F). Each seat has armrests but the centre ones don't retract for if they did, passengers could spread out to occupy both seats for a more enjoyable ride especially when trying to sleep. Helpful train crew distribute blankets to passengers in the evening. Because of the remoteness of this journey there is no wi-fi and limited mobile phone services. Each carriage has a water fountain, separate male and female toilets plus a shower but towels aren't provided.

The train crew of four make available complimentary tablets for passengers to watch movies during the journey. Meals are included in the ticket price. Snacks are available at other times with beer and wine being served along with non-alcoholic beverages. Self-service, complimentary tea and coffee is available in the lounge car, which has eight seats and six tables. There are several power points for charging electrical devices.

A locomotive crew of two changes twice along the way at Hughenden and Cloncurry. They are employed by freight company Aurizon and now just operate the three passenger carriages as post and freight are no longer carried. The engine reaches a maximum speed of 80 km/h (50 mph) although on most sections the speed is 60 km/h (37 mph) and much slower through sidings. High ambient temperatures also affect the train's speed due to the steel sleepers. It must slow down to 40 km/h (25 mph) when temperatures are high.

It's a single track all the way to Mount Isa although there are sidings to enable trains to pass. Other trains on the track are mostly those hauling minerals of copper and lead from Mount Isa, fertilizer ingredients and finished products to and from Phosphate Hill, and occasional trains transporting livestock.

THE JOURNEY

The Inlander departs Townsville, heads south to Reid River, then south-west to Charters Towers and on to Burra before tracking west to Mount Isa. The main stations are Charters Towers, Pentland,

Torrens Creek, Hughenden, Richmond, Julia Creek, Cloncurry, Duchess and Mount Isa but stops are only made when passengers need to get on or off.

Many rivers are crossed and while most are dry, during the wet season (December to March), the service can be affected by swollen rivers, although flood conditions are normally known before the train sets off.

Much of the journey passes farmland or scrubby eucalyptus forests and while without stunning features, it's forever changing. There are few settlements and even those don't amount to much. Gold was discovered in Charters Towers in 1871 and it became Queensland's second largest city with 65 hotels and a regional stock exchange. When mining declined, towns like this survived as service centres for surrounding cattle properties.

At Pentland, red soil and red-barked eucalyptus trees dot the landscape while cattle graze on the sparse grasses punctuated by termite mounds standing like sentinels on the parched earth. Gold was discovered in nearby Cape River and the railway arrived in Pentland in 1884.

Rolling hills covered in native grasses are passed in places like Praire; once a major stop for Cobb & Co. coaches. Isolated trees such as gums, mallees and acacias are scattered across the landscape.

Afterwards near Warrigal, the summer sun is almost set by 7 p.m. and at 8 p.m., there's a change of drivers in the darkness of the deserted Hughenden station. The surrounding rocks here are fossil-rich including those of dinosaurs.

While the train passes through Cloncurry in the dark, it travels in daylight on the return journey. Like Mount Isa, Cloncurry was settled in 1867 when minerals were discovered. While the railway arrived in 1907, Cloncurry also has a strong aviation connection through its association with the beginnings of Qantas, Australia's national carrier. Contestants in great air races stopped here, it was an American base during the Second World War and Australia's Royal Flying Doctor Service was established here in 1928.

The town's mining history is evident at the Chinese and Afghan Cemeteries. Cloncurry was a 'Ghantown' (abbreviation for Afghanistan) where camel herders from Afghanistan, Kashmir, Pakistan and Baluchistan lived. Some 200 cameleers and 2,000 camels provided vital regional transportation during the pioneering days. Cloncurry also has a strong association with the sheep and cattle industries.

Maldon was once a busy rail siding on the Great Northern Railway line to Mount Isa and a branch line went from Maldon

to Kuridala then on to Selwyn. Duchess is a speck on the map but a former mining hamlet where the stories in the local pub run as freely as the chilled beer.

While the local Kalkadoon Aboriginal people lived here well before the Europeans arrived, this part of inland Queensland was unknown to the outside world until 1923 when a lone prospector discovered minerals beside the Leichhardt River. Little did John Campbell Miles know but his discovery lead to the development of one of Australia's largest mines on one of the world's richest ore deposits. Visitors become aware of this as the train pulls into Mount Isa Station immediately opposite Mount Isa Mines (MIM),

now part of Glencore International, a global diversified natural resource commodity company. Several smoke stacks line the horizon with the tallest being 273 m (986 ft) high.

Outback at Isa is the best place to head for visitors with limited time as there is a mining display, an Outback Botanical Garden, the Mount Isa Regional Art Gallery and the Hard Times Mine Tour, which takes in a purpose-built mine 23 m (675 ft) underground. Included here is the Riversleigh Fossil Centre Museum (Riversleigh is a UNESCO World Heritage Site 350 km (217 miles) from Mount Isa and known amongst palaeontologists as one of the world's richest fossil sites). Mount Isa Underground Hospital and Museum behind the hospital showcase the facility built during the Second World War and a tent house where miners stayed in the pioneering days. It isn't only located in a remote part of the world but it's also hot and parched here (a high of 53.1°C/127.6°F was reached in 1889).

Returning trains to Townsville depart on the same day just after midday while coaches also travel through Mount Isa to Brisbane and Alice Springs (NT) for Adelaide (SA) or Darwin (NT).

Above: While the inland sections of the journey are through a semi-arid landscape, many rivers become swollen after monsoonal storms.

KURANDA SCENIC RAILWAY

JOURNEY THROUGH WORLD HERITAGE RAINFOREST

The 37-km (23-mile) long journey that takes almost two hours of meandering up the escarpment behind Cairns in Tropical North Queensland is one of the most popular train journeys in the whole of Australia and an essential activity for those who visit the region. While most visitors fly into Cairns International Airport for a maritime encounter on the Great Barrier Reef, the Kuranda Scenic Railway is one of several other must-do activities in a city that is well-equipped to cater to international visitors. Passengers can not only appreciate the opportunity to ride in heritage carriages but also discover the natural beauty of a UNESCO World Heritage-listed rainforest that dates back millions of years and enjoy all that the village of Kuranda has to offer.

In days past, when miners in Herberton and Mareeba on the Atherton Tablelands needed a link to the coast, a railway to Cairns was seen as the solution. Between 1882 and 1891 the Cairns to Kuranda Railway was identified and constructed (work started in 1886). It required an engineering feat of great magnitude as the track had to be excavated along steep terrain and tunnels had to be cut through the rock.

It took 1,500 workers, armed with little more than picks and shovels plus some assistance from dynamite, nine years to forge across the harsh landscape. The line was completed on June 15, 1891 and just ten days later the first passenger train operated by Kuranda Scenic Railway arrived into Kuranda. The line eventually continued and reached Ravenshoe on the Atherton Tablelands in 1916.

Trains depart from Cairns at 8.30 a.m. and 9.30 a.m. and Freshwater 20 minutes later. Return journeys depart Kuranda

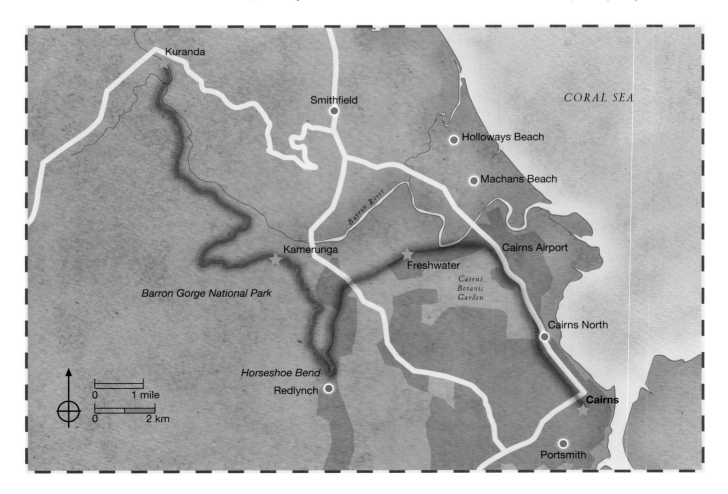

Above: Kuranda Railway Station features lush tropical plants and is considered one of Australia's most picturesque stations.

Top: On sections of the journey, passengers get a real sense of the lush tropical rainforest that the train passes so closely by.

at 2 p.m. and 3.30 p.m. Tickets in Heritage and Gold Classes are sold as are various packages that include some associated activities in Kuranda.

THE TRAIN

Red wooden carriages (some up to 100 years old) are hauled by two 1720 class diesel locomotives decorated in indigenous Buda-dji (a carpet snake) colours. These locomotives were built at Commonwealth Engineering in Rocklea, Brisbane under contract from the Clyde Engineering Company between 1966 and 1970. The service, which operates on narrow gauge (1,070 mm / 3 foot 6 inch), has access to 16 rail carriages but not all are used on any one train.

Two different classes of travel are available with Heritage Class offering an experience in refurbished vintage carriages. Gold Class offers extra comfort and luxury. The restored carriages whose cedar interiors have individual lounge chairs are adorned with historical photos and each has a dedicated train assistant. The welcome starts with a tropical mocktail at Freshwater Station. Along the way, passengers are served locally grown produce from Cairns, Kuranda and the Atherton Tablelands including Gallo Dairyland Cheese, Skybury Coffee, Daintree Tea and super-crisp lager from the Great Northern Brewing Company. An exclusive tour of the heritage-listed signal cabin at Kuranda Station is also offered.

THE JOURNEY

Trains depart from Cairns Station located beneath Cairns Central Shopping Centre in the city centre. A comprehensive trip guide in nine different languages is provided with ticket purchase and onboard announcements are made in English.

A route north-west out of Cairns is followed before the train passes Cairns International Airport and heads inland (westwards). Its first stop is Freshwater Station where many passengers board the train. Freshwater Station was built to characterize the history of the region and the railway. It was important for the railway's construction crews as they were assured good drinking water from the nearby Barron River.

Within a few kilometres of departing Freshwater, Redlynch and Jungara (once the site of largest field hospital in the southern hemisphere during the Second World War), the train moves out of the valley and begins the slow climb of the escarpment. At Horseshoe Bend, the train makes an 180-degree turn with passengers at the rear and right-hand side of the train having the best location for photography.

On its journey up the escarpment, the train meanders past waterfalls, 15 hand-hewn tunnels and 37 bridges through the Barron Gorge National Park and into Kuranda.

Tunnel number six has special notoriety due to the daring daylight rail hold-up made in 1972 by masked bandits. They escaped through the rugged and dense rainforest on trail bikes with money that was destined for the tablelands to pay wages. They have never been brought to justice.

Despite it now being a mere blip along the route, Stoney Creek Station was once a busy settlement with pubs, amusement halls and even a Methodist Church when the line was being built. The railway continues on to what is considered the masterpiece of the railway; the bridge across Stoney Creek and its waterfall. Completed in the mid 1860s and made from iron latticework, it is supported by three trestle piers. With a tight radius, the train passes slowly over the curved bridge within metres of the falls on the left-hand side of the train making for a spectacular sight.

Possibly the best elevated panorama of the lowland below is viewed just after the bridge and tunnel 14, on the train's right-hand side. Quick glimpses of the Coral Sea, the Great Barrier Reef and Cairns can be seen between the enveloping rainforest beside the track. Much of the rainforest in the far north is World Heritage listed with the UNESCO site being known as the Wet Tropics of Queensland. These forests contain a vast assemblage of plants (12,000 flowering plants) including 715 species found nowhere else in the world. Some 336 birds have been identified here including the large cassowary.

The train continues to wind through lush rainforest framed by rugged mountains and waterfalls that cascade into deep ravines. Barron Falls warrants a ten-minute stop at a viaduct that also serves as a station and viewing platform. The local indigenous people believe that Buda-dji, the Carpet Snake, carved out the Barron River and its tributaries.

Passengers can alight here onto the platform and viewing deck some 329 m (1,079 ft) above the lowlands to admire the cascading Barron Falls which drop 265 m (869 ft) into the Barron River Valley.

Kuranda Station as it stands today only opened in 1915 and the Kuranda Tea Room here is an essential stop for refreshments and souvenirs. The station is arguably one of the most beautiful in Australia with its lush tropical landscaping and heritage-listed Federation style architecture. Its signal cabin is one of just nine remaining hand-lever operations in the state.

Kuranda is just a short walk from the station. Its tranquillity

appeals to those seeking an alternative lifestyle and it first captured the attention of hippies in the 1960s. Subsequently artisans, craftspeople and new-agers settled here. Many come to wander the streets and to explore the Original Markets or the newer Heritage Markets. Village and regional attractions now offer a more comprehensive and diverse range of activities including the Rainforestation Nature Park (also home to the Pamagirri Dancers), Birdworld, the Australian Butterfly Sanctuary and Koala Gardens. Many visitors arrive on the first train, explore the village and then return on the last train.

Another popular alternative is to experience the Skyrail Rainforest Cableway back down the escarpment to its terminus near Smithfield. This is an exhilarating glide above and through the rainforest canopy recognized internationally as one of the oldest continually surviving rainforests on earth. Dreamtime at Tjapukai Aboriginal Cultural Park is located nearby.

Above: While some visitors to Kuranda return to Cairns on the train, others take the exhilarating Skyrail Rainforest Cableway down the escarpment.

Opposite: The train stops on the Stoney Creek bridge for passengers to alight and photograph the forests and waterfalls.

TASMANIA

INTRODUCTION

Australia's smallest and only island state covers 67,800 sq km (26,178 sq miles) or approximately one per cent of the total country. It was initially known as Van Diemen's Land (named by the Dutch in 1642 while charting parts of the island), became an independent colony in 1825 and was proclaimed Tasmania in 1855. In 1803, Hobart Town was established as the first European settlement on the island and the second in Australia. It started as a penal colony and a defensive outpost as the French were exploring the region and contemplating expanding their empire. The Macquarie Harbour Penal Station on Sarah Island in the isolated south-west was reserved for the worst convicts. In 1804, the settlement relocated to its present site of Constitution Dock and Salamanca Place.

One of the first rail lines in Australia entered service at Port Arthur in 1836 as a convict-hauled conveyance along fixed parallel rails across the Tasman Peninsula. It has been documented that on sections of the 7-km (4⅓-mile) journey, speeds of 40 km/h (25 mph) were achieved.

Tasmania has a mountainous interior and many parts are covered in dense temperate rainforests, not ideal railway country therefore. It is rich in minerals and extracting them in the early days was mostly done via horse-drawn wagons hauled along iron rails and wooden sleepers. Some were privately owned with little or no connectivity between them to enable passengers to move from one to another.

In 1871, the first steam train started operations as the Launceston to Deloraine Railway between the two towns. A year later, Tasmanian Government Railways was formed and was in existence until 1978 when it was absorbed into the Australian National Railway Commission and operated as Tasrail. Freight trains still operate on parts of the island where, at one stage, there were 16 lines and 275 stations.

Of all the Australian states, Tasmania is possibly the one where motor vehicles have had the greatest impact on rail travel. As more people started to drive, fewer passengers travelled on the rail and today, there are no scheduled passenger trains operating in Tasmania but there are tourist trains and museums to explore including the West Coast Wilderness Train, Wee Georgie Wood, Redwater Creek Steam and Heritage Society, Don River Railway, Derwent Valley Railway, Launceston Tramway Museum, Tasmanian Transport Museum and Ida Bay Railway.

Wee Georgie Wood Railway operates in Tullah on the last weekend of the month from October to June. It is the only 610 mm (2 foot) gauge, steam railway operating on Tasmania's West Coast. The original track laid down here in 1902 was a horse-drawn railway into Tullah, which only became accessible by road in 1963. However, by then, the horses had been replaced by an 'iron horse'.

Redwater Creek Steam and Heritage Society operate a steam train on the first weekend of the month from their Sheffield Station base between 11 a.m. and 4 p.m. It offers a 2-km (1-mile) trip on a steam train. Steamfest Sheffield is staged in March as Tasmania's largest gathering of working steam-powered equipment.

Launceston Tramway Museum is open from Monday to Saturday daily from 10 a.m. until 4 p.m. The tram operates from Wednesday to Saturday with a soundscape featuring sounds and voices from the past. The museum is located in the former Inveresk Railway Yards in Launceston.

The Tasmanian Transport Museum in Glenorchy is open at the weekends from 1 p.m. to 5 p.m. with rides available on the first and third Sundays of the month. Visitors can inspect a large collection of trains, trams and buses.

Ida Bay Railway operates three journeys daily using a Second World War diesel locomotive along a 7-km (4⅓-mile) track located 105 km (65 miles) south of Hobart. The Railway offers a two-hour return journey on the original 610 mm (2 foot) gauge bush tramway to a secluded beach.

There are other train-related activities and groups in the island state including the Derwent Valley Railway at New Norfolk and Evandale Light Railway and Steam Society.

Opposite: One of the three beautifully restored Abt steam trains en route from Queenstown.

THE WEST COAST WILDERNESS TRAIN

A JOURNEY THROUGH ANCIENT RAINFORESTS

Tasmania's mountainous West Coast is sparsely settled and covered in lush temperate rainforests dissected by wild rivers. It is here that the West Coast Wilderness Railway operates as a restoration of the original Mount Lyell Mining and Railway Company Limited service from Queenstown to Strahan (Regatta Point) on the far west coast of the island. The next landfall is Antarctica beyond the vast expanse of the windswept Southern Ocean.

When construction started on the 1,067 mm (3 foot 6 inch) gauge railway in 1895, Tasmania's west coast was one of the most remote parts of the world and, even today, not much has changed. Despite roads connecting Queenstown and Strahan to civilization, such as Hobart, the state capital, there's still a sense of entering the lost world once the train ventures into the lush temperate forests along the 35-km (22-mile) route.

The discovery of copper in Queenstown was one thing; getting the copper concentrate to the port of Strahan and market was another. A route was identified through the mountainous topography of the steep ravines of the King River and the

Above: The builder's plate showing that this diesel locomotive was constructed by The Vulcan Foundry in Lancashire, England in 1953.

Opposite: An original Mount Lyell Drewry 0-6-0 diesel locomotive is coupled to the train for the final section of the track into Regatta Point.

Following pages: The West Coast Wilderness Train taking on water.

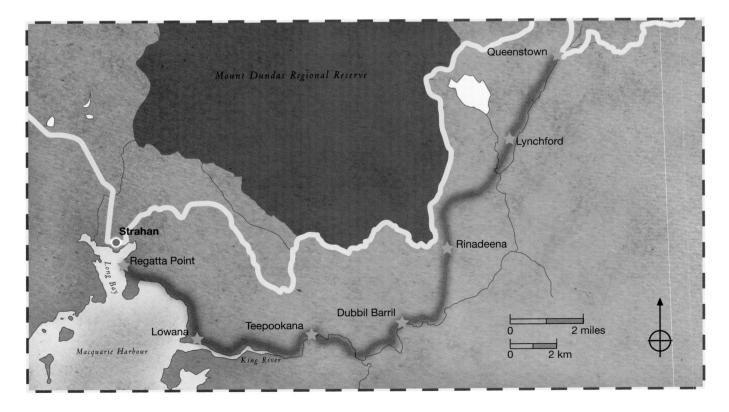

dense rainforest. Some 500 labourers worked in dangerous conditions on the railway, taking two-and-a-half years to clear a route through the rainforest. The summers were steaming hot and the winters cold and wet. Reports indicate that only two labourers died in the railway's construction and that the authorities appeared surprised that the figure was so low. Fettlers and their families lived in makeshift camps to maintain the line once it was constructed.

When the train commenced service in 1897 it was lauded as a magnificent engineering feat. The railway crossed 60 timber bridges of stepped trestles with the extension from Teepookana to Strahan being completed in 1900. The original railway remained in service for 67 years, whereas the first road only connected Queenstown to the outside world in 1932.

An Abt rack-and-pinion system was incorporated into sections of the line to enable trains to haul heavy loads up the steep terrain (1:16). Five engines eventually operated on the line and it was one of only two such systems to be established in Australia (the other operated at Mount Morgan in Queensland). The system (with solid bars and vertical teeth) was invented by Swiss engineer, Dr

Roman Abt and first used in Harzbahn, Germany in 1885. The 'teeth' in the middle of the rails engaged with a small cogwheel underneath the locomotive to 'drag' it up hills while acting as a brake on the downhill sections.

The railway survived floods, bushfires and wash-outs. However, by 1963 rising track-maintenance bills forced the mining company to resort to using trucks to transport the copper by road to Strahan. The railway fell into disrepair until 1999 when a restoration proposal was suggested and accepted. Bushfires, floods and natural attrition had further taken their toll and the stations had all disappeared apart from Regatta Point and a section of Queenstown. The five trains were also in various states of disrepair and scattered around Tasmania and the Australian mainland.

After a significant injection of funds, the track and infrastructure were restored and a section of the railway reopened in 2000. The new train features purpose-built carriages fitted out with Tasmanian timbers and modelled along the lines of the original Mount Lyell carriages. In December 2003, the full service from Queenstown to Strahan was reintroduced after a three-year restoration programme.

There are various departures depending upon the season with a popular journey leaving from Queenstown in the morning. It follows the Queen River before reaching Halls Creek Siding where the rack-and-pinion system is put in place. The section from Halls Creek to Rindadeena Saddle attains gradients of 1:16 or 6.2 per cent and passengers soon appreciate the importance of the Abt system. Just prior to reaching Dubbil Barril and the end of the rack-and-pinion system, the train passes the picturesque King River Gorge. The route closely follows the river down to Lowana where the King River meets the vast Macquarie Harbour. Now on flat ground, the line heads north all the way to Regatta Point on the outskirts of the coastal village of Strahan.

Passengers have three journeys from which to choose – the Rack and Gorge (Queenstown – Dubbil Barril – Queenstown), River and Rainforest (Strahan – Dubbil Barril – Strahan) and the Queenstown Explorer (Strahan – Queenstown – Strahan). The first two are half-day journeys while the last is a full-day experience. Two types of tickets are sold with a standard fare in a Heritage Carriage or in a Wilderness Carriage, which includes a glass of Tasmanian sparkling wine for which the state is famous, an open-air balcony section at the end of the carriage affording great views and photo opportunities, plus morning tea, lunch or afternoon tea (depending upon the experience booked and the time of day).

A new service offering rafting as part of the train journey operates every Thursday from November to mid-April. Guides from the King River Rafting Company lead rafters on an exhilarating journey that departs from Queenstown and descends through the King River Gorge and its thrilling rapids to emerge at Sailor Jack Creek and the Rhododendron Pool. They reboard the train at Dubbil Barril Station for the return train journey to Queenstown.

Passengers departing from Queenstown can enjoy refreshments in the Tracks Café before departure, browse through the Railway Gift Shop for train-related literature and excellent Tasmanian produce or learn more about the train in the Abt Railway Museum. Catering features fresh Tasmanian produce and the island's finest beers, wines and other beverages.

There are five stops along the journey: Lynchford, Rinadeena, Dubbil Barril, Lower Landing/Teepookana and Lowana. Activities at the stations, such as gold panning and a rainforest walk add to the journey's excitement. Tasting Tasmania's unique leatherwood honey from hives located in the Teepookana Plateau rainforests is another highlight. One of the most scenic sections is through the 163-m (500-ft) deep King River Gorge, where the train passes along an embankment 65 m (200 ft) above the wilderness river rushing below.

Three Abt steam trains are used from Queenstown and include Abt 1 dating back to 1896, Abt 3 (1898) and Abt 5 (1938). The railway also operates two original Mount Lyell Drewery 0-6-0 diesel locomotives on the rare occasions when steam trains cannot be used. Regatta Point is a short distance from the village best known as the departure point for boat cruises on Macquarie Harbour and the UNESCO World Heritage Site of the Gordon River.

Now revitalized as a tourist train, the West Coast Wilderness Railway is one steam train that simply refuses to die.

Above: The final stretch of the line skirts the coast before reaching the terminal at Regatta Point near Strahan.

Opposite: The scenery along the journey features wild rivers and untouched forests. Trains travel slowly enough to allow photography.

THE DON RIVER RAILWAY

RECREATING TASMANIAN RAILWAY HISTORY

This railway, based in Devonport in northern Tasmania, is operated by the Van Diemen Light Railway Society, a dedicated group of volunteers and enthusiasts. The society's aim is to preserve a representative selection of former Tasmanian railway equipment. Don River Railway has Tasmania's largest collection of steam locomotives dating from 1879 to 1951. It also has Tasmania's most extensive collection of passenger carriages, which date from 1869 to 1964.

In addition to a small operational train line, there is a workshop and former railway station that operates as a ticket office and souvenir shop. All are accessed from Forth Main Road just off the Bass Highway and five minutes to the west of the ferry terminal (Devonport to Melbourne) or 15 minutes from Devonport Airport.

In 1854, a timber mill and wharf were built on the west bank of the Don River and a tramway to carry extracted timber from the valley followed. From 1862, coal was also transported from a small mine located nearby. In 1873, the Don River Company built a new 1,372 mm (4 foot 6 inch) gauge track to replace the tramway. The line was worked by horses and a steam locomotive but was abandoned by the 1880s. It was revitalized when limestone (used as a flux in the blast furnaces of the steelworks in Newcastle, New South Wales) was quarried in Melrose just south of Don. A branch line to Melrose opened in 1916 to accommodate trains servicing the quarry, carrying general freight and providing some passenger services. Movements peaked just before the Second World War but traffic declined afterwards when the quarry closed and general traffic dwindled prior to the line being closed in 1963. In 1964, the rail line from Don to Melrose was lifted but the 3.5-km (2¼-mile) track from Don to Don Junction was retained. Trains currently operate on this track from Wednesday to Sunday and special concessions are available for groups, while steam locomotive journeys can be arranged for large groups.

THE TRAIN

The Don River Railway provides an opportunity to ride on a genuine vintage train along the old Melrose line to Coles Beach and back. The Railway has a collection of steam and diesel locomotives, restored carriages and railway equipment. Its steam train collection includes M class number 4, H class number 7 (entered service in

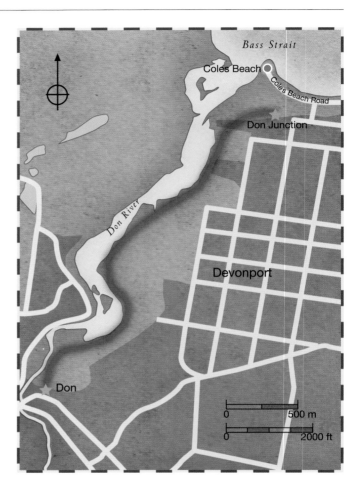

1952 as the last steam train acquired by Tasmanian Government Railway), a Fowler steam locomotive built in 1886 and a Heemskirk number 8. Passengers will, however, mostly ride on one of the diesel locomotives or railcars such as DP22 (built by Waddingtons of Sydney in 1939) or EBR 10 class (ex Emu Bay Railways and built by Walkers Limited in Maryborough, Queensland).

There are a dozen or so restored carriages including one of the most recent additions, the carriage numbered DB5. Another unusual carriage is the Riley Rail Car number 1 while the Royal Carriage is the grandest. The latter dates back to 1879 and was purchased by the society in 1982. In 2009, a decision was made to transform the carriage and restore it to the style as used by the British Royal Family when they visited Tasmania.

THE JOURNEY

The train operates daily except for Good Friday and Christmas Day with trains departing Don on the hour between 10 a.m. and 4 p.m. for the 30-minute journey along the forested eastern riverbank of the Don River. It is worth arriving early to inspect the

memorabilia and model trains in the old railway station office. This is not the original station but is the former Ulverstone Railway Station building, which was acquired, dismantled, relocated and rebuilt by the society. The signal box is the original from Devonport Railway Station and there is a turntable that was relocated from Anthill in southern Tasmania.

The tourist train has travelled along the tracks of the former Melrose line since 1976 to offer passengers a short scenic journey through the forested area.

Coles Beach is a short walk from the terminus at Don Junction, which faces Bass Strait near the mouth of the Don River. This is a beautiful and quiet part of the Devonport coastline with picnic and barbecue facilities as well as toilets and showers. Within walking distance of the beach are Mersey Bluff Lighthouse and a little further, the Bass Strait Maritime Centre.

Above: Many journeys are hauled by a diesel locomotive.

Opposite: The railway has Tasmania's largest collection of steam locomotives.

NORTHERN TERRITORY

INTRODUCTION

The Northern Territory is best known as the 'Top End' with its inland Outback parts called the 'Red Centre' after the unique and ever-changing colours of the landscape. While a vast territory covering 1.3 million sq km (520, 902 sq miles), it is sparsely populated with fewer than 250,000 residents.

Beyond the tropical and monsoonal north, the rest of the state is mostly desert or semi-desert and home to vast cattle ranches, some of which are the size of countries with seats in the United Nations (Alexandria Station, for example, is almost as big as Kuwait).

The first European settlers arrived in 1869 in what was then called Palmerston and is now the capital, Darwin. It took weeks for supplies to arrive by ship and interest in a rail connection to the south, started early in the history of the territory.

Things improved and Australia became more connected to the outside world when the 3,200-km (1,988-mile) long Overland Telegraph was forged through the Australian Outback from South Australia to Darwin between 1870 and 1872. This linked to an underwater cable between Java in Indonesia and Europe. What is significant about the telegraph route is that it opened up the possibility of a rail connection and the famous Afghan cameleers helped supply those erecting the overland telegraph.

GOLD, GOLD, GOLD

In 1871 during construction of the telegraph line, gold was unearthed at a place called Pine Creek. This resulted in a gold rush not dissimilar to those in the other Australian colonies and soon the small settlement grew to a population of 3,000 (five times its existing

population). Fifteen mines were quarried. The feverish mining activity continued when tin was discovered in 1878.

The first rail line in the north was that between Port Darwin and Pine Creek on what was known as the North Australia Railway. It arrived in Pine Creek in 1888 and it was envisaged that it would ultimately join with the one that was slowly being built north from South Australia. It helped that the Northern Territory was then administered by South Australia.

The contract for the line was awarded to a Melbourne company on the proviso that 'coolie' labour could be used. Both Chinese and Indian workers were used to lay the tracks and build the bridges for the 243-km (145-mile) long railway line. For many, this railway link was seen as only the beginning with the ultimate goal being to connect the line all the way south to Adelaide.

In 1911, the Northern Territory fell under the control of the Commonwealth and some years later the line was extended through to Emungalen on the banks of the Katherine River and just north of Katherine. Plans were in place to extend the line to Daly Waters but funds ran out during the Depression and the line terminated in Birdum, which was nothing more than the end of the track in the semi-arid north 509 km (316 miles) south of Darwin.

BRIDGING THE GAP

During the Second World War, Darwin became one of the few places in Australian to be directly attacked by the Japanese. Unlike Queensland, there was no rail link beyond Alice Springs thus hampering the movement of troops from the populated southern parts of Australia to the north where the biggest threat of invasion or attack existed. The link between Port Augusta and Darwin was made an all-weather road during the war and many airstrips were built. After the bombing of Darwin, civilians were evacuated by rail to Birdum and then put on an army convoy to Alice Springs. Some one million United States personnel passed through Australia during the Second World War with many concentrated in northern Australia near the Pacific theatre of war. The Defence of Darwin in the Darwin Military Museum documents the city's pivotal role during the war.

While a rail link was also considered important for the defence of the nation, it wasn't until much later that the four-year construction of the railway line commenced. On July 17, 2001, the first piece of earth was finally turned for the 1,420-km (882-mile) rail link between Alice Springs and Darwin. The shovel used in this ceremony was a nickel-plated one borrowed from the Australian Museum and

first used in 1878 by the then South Australian Governor for the start of what was to be a transcontinental line to the north.

Rail visitors to the Northern Territory are more likely to see 'road' trains of elongated trucks on the highways than trains on the railways. Visitors can catch *The Ghan* to Alice Springs and use it as a base to explore attractions such as Ayers Rock (Uluru), The Olgas and the MacDonnell Ranges but the vast distances of the north mean that other forms of transportation are required.

Above: *The Ghan* enables passengers to admire Australia's 'Red Centre'.

Opposite: The Northern Territory's first railway was from Port Darwin (pictured) to Pine Creek.

THE GHAN: DARWIN TO ADELAIDE

NORTH TO SOUTH THROUGH AUSTRALIA'S RED CENTRE

The Ghan that connects Darwin in the Northern Territory to Adelaide in South Australia is one of the world's best-known railway journeys and epic odysseys. Extending over 2,979 km (1,858 miles), it is the second longest rail journey in Australia after the *Indian Pacific*.

The majority of Australia's 23.2 million citizens live around the coastline of this vast continent. The main concentration is around the south-east from Sydney to Melbourne. Beyond the fertile coast, there are very few built-up areas in what is known to many as 'The Outback'. Further inland is the Red Centre with its dramatic but parched arid landscapes, where skies laden with stars provide a moonscape like nothing else on Earth. Access to Australia's Outback has never been easy and communications were, and still are in some areas, just as difficult. Scotsman John McDouall Stuart completed the first known north-to-south crossing over the arid continent in 1862.

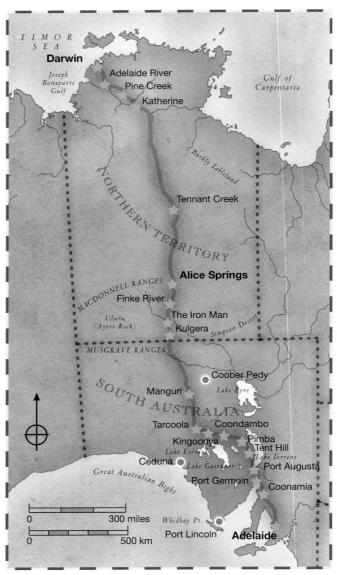

Above: One of the optional extras when travelling on *The Ghan* is to go on a camel ride from Alice Springs and to have sweeping views across the MacDonnell Ranges.

Opposite: The longest *Ghan* train comprised 44 carriages and two locomotives; a distance of 1,096 m (3,596 ft).

Camels and camel drivers from Afghanistan (and several neighbouring countries) were brought to Australia to transport provisions for the line's construction along the desolate and treacherous inland route. Cameleers and their camels were also on hand in 1878 to assist with the construction of the train line north from Port Augusta and closely following Stuart's route. However, it wasn't until 1929 that Adelaide was connected by railway to the town called Stuart (now Alice Springs) in the Northern Territory.

Above: *The Ghan* is one of Australia's two trans-continental railway journeys.

Top: The Afghan cameleers and their camels who helped construct the track and gave the train its name.

Opposite: Departures on *The Ghan* are weekly, leaving Darwin on Wednesdays and Adelaide on Sundays.

The line was extended by Commonwealth Railways, later renamed Central Australia Railway. Volumes have been written about the long and protracted construction of the railway.

In 1883, an ambitious North Australia Railway forged southwards from Palmerston (near Darwin) with the long-term vision of linking with the line heading north from South Australia. The southern line eventually reached and stopped in Alice Springs, while the line tracking down from the north only reached and provided access to settlements such as Adelaide River, Palmerston, Pine Creek and Katherine but wasn't connected to Alice Springs until many decades later.

Both railway lines were narrow gauge lines of 1,067 mm (3 foot 6 inch) but this was progressively changed in the south starting in 1957 to a standard 1,435 mm (4 foot 8½ inch) gauge. The standard gauge was extended through to Alice Springs in 1980 but it wasn't until February 2004 that the line eventually connected Alice Springs to Darwin in the north.

The Ghan is an abbreviation for *Afghan Express* and was used in preference to the Central Australia Railway, which officially started operations in August 1929. Steam trains ceased operating to Alice Springs in 1951, when they were replaced by diesel-electric locomotives. Because the steam trains needed water, the original route was carefully plotted to pass remote desert locations where precious water could be sourced from artesian bores. When the new line opened in 1980 for diesel locomotive use, the need for water was no longer paramount and the new track was installed 160 km (100 miles) to the west of the original route.

The Ghan now operates along the line from Darwin to Adelaide and vice versa with the standard trip lasting three days and two nights (54 hours) with a new four-day, three-night journey having just been introduced seasonally on the Darwin to Adelaide route only.

Most passengers are amazed at the length of the 30-carriage train, which is normally 710 m (2,329 ft) long inclusive of two diesels (National Pacific NR class locomotives along with AN and DL classes), guest and crew carriages, restaurants, bars, power van and car transporter carriages (vehicles can also be carried on the train). It operates at an average speed of 85 km/h (53 mph) and a maximum of 115 km/h (71 mph). On each journey, it consumes 40,000 litres (10,560 gallons) of diesel fuel and each carriage carries 3,000 litres (793 gallons) of water. Thirty crew serve the 500 Platinum and Gold Class passengers housed in accommodation ranging from luxurious single to double cabins.

Right: Passengers are treated to all-inclusive meals and beverages in fine dining surroundings.

Below: Australia's dramatic 'Red Centre' landscape makes this one of the country's most popular railway journeys.

Opposite: The landscape in the far north of Australia is monsoonal with abundant water in the wet season and lush forests in parts.

Platinum Class passengers enjoy large private cabins, lounge seating (which converts to a double bed in the evening), en suite bathroom, and all meals of regionally-sourced produce and beverages including excellent Australian wines. The facilities are similar for those in Gold Class but with less lavish and less spacious accommodation. Both classes share the Outback Explorer Lounge and the Queen Adelaide Restaurant, while Platinum Class passengers now have exclusive access to their own lounge/dining carriage called the Platinum Class.

Despite passing through desert for much of the journey, the dramatic and ancient Australian landscape is ever-changing. Stops and complimentary off-train excursions are conducted at Katherine and Alice Springs with the quirky underground opal mining settlement of Coober Pedy being a new destination on the four-day journey. Passengers on the standard southern journey board the train on Wednesday morning and pass through the lush Top End before arriving in Katherine after lunch. Here, passengers can visit Nitmiluk Gorge and cruise on the picturesque Katherine River or attend the Katherine Outback Experience stockman show before a late afternoon departure (from late May to late August, there is an additional departure from Darwin only on Saturday and in December and January, there is one departure every fortnight).

After a journey of 1,420 km (882 miles), *The Ghan* arrives into Alice Springs located in the majestic MacDonnell Ranges just after breakfast on day two. After passengers have had time to visit the local sights, it departs in the early afternoon for the final 1,559 km (969 miles). In the evening, the train stops at Manguri near Coober Pedy for an Outback evening under the dazzling stars in a clear desert night. Adelaide is the final destination on day three with the train arriving into the South Australia capital just before noon.

While the train is air conditioned, there are several side trips from the train and for passengers, choosing the most appropriate season for them is important. Two seasons dominate central and northern Australia with the dry season (May to October) and wet season (November to April). The dry season is the most popular time to travel because the weather is cooler, humidity lower and there is usually no rain. In the wet, monsoonal rains may cut roads and close access to some off-train venues.

Great Southern Railway also operates two other iconic Australian rail journeys – the *Indian Pacific* (Perth to Sydney) and *The Overland* (Melbourne to Adelaide). While possibly overshadowed by Australia's equally famous train the *Indian Pacific*, *The Ghan* remains one of the world's great train journeys and a national Australian treasure that many aspire to travel on.

Passengers on the *Northern Explorer* can admire the ever-changing rural scenery from an open-air viewing deck and large panoramic windows.

NEW ZEALAND

THE NORTH ISLAND

INTRODUCTION

It has been documented that the first passenger carriage on the North Island was one hauled by a Chaplin engine made in Glasgow on December 4, 1871. Little is known of this train except that it was sold to the Thames Gold Mine on the southern shores of the Hauraki Gulf after it was used to carry passengers.

The most important rail line on the North Island is the Main North Trunk Line linking the capital Wellington with the largest city of Auckland (served by the *Northern Explorer*). The first section opened in 1873 in Auckland and extended 13 km (eight miles) from Point Britomart to Onehunga via Penrose. Construction at the southern or Wellington end started in 1885. The line was completed in 1908 and was operational the next year. It opened the island up for settlers and generated economic activity that was not previously possible. Initially passenger trains took 20 hours to complete the journey, which today the *Northern Explorer* does in just 11.

The Goldfields Railway Society operates from Waihi Railway Station near Paeroa to the south-east of Auckland. It was established in 1980 to preserve the local rail heritage and now operates a tourist train from Waihi to Waikino. This picturesque journey takes just 30 minutes and enables passengers to view sections of the old mining activity plus the scenic Ohinemuri River. It offers three journeys per day over the weekend as well as on public and school holidays.

One of the projects of the Railway Enthusiasts Society is the Glenbrook Vintage Railway just south of Auckland. They have an extensive collection of steam and diesel locomotives and heritage carriages.

Bush tramways are another feature of the New Zealand railway landscape. Railway tractors were commonly used on small bush tramways around the country as a more cost-effective option to operating locomotives.

One example is a bush tramway 'white' jigger that is based in Pukemiro in the Waikato region (so named because it is based upon a White truck). It once served the logging industry around Mamaku just to the north-east of Rotorua. Farm tractors, trucks and even bulldozers were modified to operate on rails with some replacing teams of horses that had previously been used. They first appeared in 1924 and remained in service until 1956. The timber industry in the Mamaku district peaked in the 1940s with some six jiggers serving 14 sawmills.

The Bush Tramway Club also operates the Glen Afton Line Heritage Railway from its Huntly base. This runs along an old section of the Glen Afton Branch Line, which served the coal mine at Pukemiro for most of its working life from 1915 to 1973. The railway has an extensive collection of steam and diesel locomotives plus jiggers and bush jiggers. While visitors are welcomed year-round, trains mostly operate along a 12-km (7½-mile) long track on the first Sunday of the month between April and December.

Left: While the track still remains, regular rail services through Kumeu, north-west of Auckland, have ceased.

Below: Passengers on the *Northern Explorer* pass close to the alpine landscape of Mount Tongariro National Park.

BAY OF ISLANDS VINTAGE RAILWAY

MAIN STREET KAWAKAWA

This vintage train has one of the longest steam-train heritages in New Zealand and operates on one of the only rail tracks in the world that runs on a state highway and along a town main street. Trains depart from Kawakawa Station on Gillies Street for Taumarere station perched at the western end of the Long Bridge; a wooden construction that crosses the Kawakawa River in the north-east of New Zealand's North Island.

The total journey is currently just 4.8 km (three miles) long, only about one-third of the original track which covers a total distance of 11.5 km (seven miles). During the trip, the train passes over eight bridges to reach Taumarere Station, one of New Zealand's oldest station buildings, where the locomotive is repositioned from the front of the train to the rear for the return journey. While this happens passengers are taken on a short guided walk to the 'Long Bridge' (bridge number nine); the longest curved wooden bridge in the southern hemisphere.

When coal was discovered in Kawakawa in 1864, an entrepreneur named John McLeod began to construct a 4.8-km (three-mile) long tramway mostly made from timber. This enabled horses to haul wooden tubs of coal down to the Kawakawa River where they were then loaded onto punts with a shallow-draught beside the banks of the Kawakawa River at Taumarere for conveyance to steam-driven ships berthed in what became the deep-sea port of Opua further downstream at the head of the Bay of Islands.

In 1867 McLeod took out a lease for the Bay of Islands Coal Company, which then employed 60 workers in an era when Taumarere was the largest town in the region. A standard gauge metal rail line was built in 1871 and the first steam engine on the

Above: Maintaining trains is a long and costly exercise but lovingly done by enthusiastic volunteers.

Opposite: Arrive early at Kawakawa Station to browse the book and souvenir shop or enjoy a break in the café beside the platform.

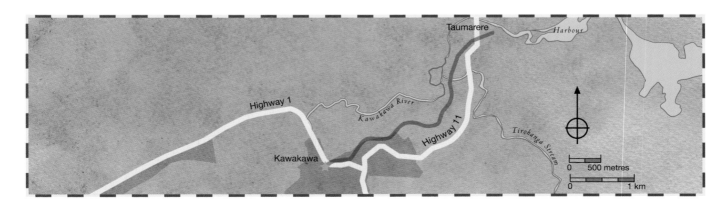

North Island ran along the line on January 28, 1871. The engine was built by Alexander Chaplin and Co. in Glasgow, Scotland and initially it hauled 7.3 tonnes (eight tons) of coal but once the engine's shortcomings were rectified, it was reputed to be able to pull 21 tonnes (23 tons).

The original locomotive was sold in late 1871 and two 0-6-0, 14.5-tonne (16-ton) Manning Wardle saddle tank engines built in Leeds, England were purchased. One, named 'Driver', was used for hauling and the other was used to pump out the mine, which suffered from flooding. These engines were purchased from the defunct Auckland to Drury Railway. 'Driver' also pulled a four-wheel based passenger carriage, built in England in 1872, which had first and second class compartments. Today, a replica carriage named 'Moa' has been built and is used by the railway.

On February 22, 1877, the 1,070 mm (3 foot 6 inch) gauge was implemented across the county. By 1878, the loading and unloading of coal became more mechanized and efficient at Derrick Landing, Taumarere, as a crane lifted the coal boxes from the train and the coal was released via a trapdoor into the awaiting barges moored along the riverbank. Two paddle steamers named 'Ida' and 'Black

Diamond' pulled the barges down the river to its junction with the Waikare River.

On April 7, 1884, the Long Bridge and rail extension to the deep-sea port of Opua were opened (the port was previously named One Tree Point and Newport). However, from 1899, mining was scaled back and the coal was only used locally.

Railway sleepers and piles for bridge construction on the line are made from Australian hardwood sourced from jarrah trees. These were used in the Kawakawa to Towai extension completed on July 10, 1910, which joined the line from Opua to Whangarei. Kawakawa Station was only opened in 1911. By 1921, frozen meat was being exported to the United Kingdom from Opua, which by this stage was a busy port for exporting local produce and products. However, exports from Opua declined and the line from Kawakawa to Opua eventually closed in 1985. In the same year the Bay of Islands Scenic Railway was established to operate a scenic tourist railway on the same section of track. The locomotive 'Gabriel' was initially loaned to the railway by Portland Cement situated in Whangarei. An enthusiast and member of the Opua and Kawakawa Rail Preservation Society

then purchased the engine before donating it to the Bay of Islands Scenic Railway.

There was a lapse in tourist services between 2000 and 2006 when the line was reopened and operated by the Bay of Islands Vintage Railway Trust. Plans are in place to complete the re-piling of the Long Bridge and continue the line through to Opua, the full 11.5 km (seven miles) and an hour-long trip.

The train is staffed by volunteers, and enthusiasts are welcome to become involved by supporting or funding their efforts through the Gabriel Club.

THE TRAIN
'Gabriel', the class 4-4-0 steam locomotive number 1730 built by Peckett and Sons in Bristol, is the railway's big attraction. This side-tank steam engine was built in 1927, and is the only one of its class remaining in the world. While 'Gabriel' is regularly used and is everybody's favourite, one of the five vintage diesel locomotives is also used as a replacement when the steam locomotive is in the workshop. The first two were delivered to Southern Ireland, two to Sarawak on the island of Borneo, and the last one to Portland Cement in Whangarei. In Whangarei it was used to move coal and

lime wagons around the cement works. The normal train configuration consists of three carriages including a converted open goods wagon used mostly for the transportation of 25 bicycles but with standing room for passengers, a fully-enclosed passenger carriage and a semi-open observation car at the rear.

The open-sided observation car is especially popular as it offers the best location for photography and for taking in the fresh rural air. Four wooden seats are positioned parallel to the rails for an uninterrupted view of the passing countryside, although passengers can also stand along the sides. Windows on the enclosed carriage are small but they partially open to allow a little of the outside into the carriage.

THE JOURNEY
There are four departures a day year-round on Fridays, Saturdays and Sundays with a diesel locomotive being used on Fridays and the steam engine on most Saturdays and Sundays, although this is subject to variation mostly based upon the serviceability of the steam locomotive, which is some 90 years old. There are also departures every day on school and public holidays (steam on Fridays to Mondays and diesel on Tuesdays to Thursdays).

Departures from Kawakawa leave at 10.45 a.m., noon, 1.30 p.m. and 3 p.m. Trains depart from Taumarere at 11.15 a.m., 12.30 p.m. 1.45 p.m. and 3 p.m. Special charters can also be arranged outside of scheduled departures. The round trip only takes 45 minutes.

The journey commences from Kawakawa Station with the clang of a bell, a whistle blast from the guard and a toot from the locomotive. Immediately it passes a road crossing and then travels down the centre of the main street.

Passengers and well-wishers along both sides of the street wave enthusiastically especially those photographing the town's other main attraction; the Hundertwasser public toilets. These are not just *any* toilets but those designed by the famous Austrian artist Frederick Stowasser Hundertwasser, who relocated from Vienna to the town after falling in love with it after a visit. Hundertwasser became a New Zealand citizen who not only paid towards the purchase and restoration of the rail carriage

named 'Pukeko' and acted as a great friend to the railway, but also created possibly the world's most artistic and colourful toilets. They are famous amongst fans of his quirky artistic style as they are his last work.

As the train travels slowly down the main street, the guard waves down cars that need to stop to allow the train to pass safely along the street. Once it is out of the town limits the landscape is mostly lush rolling hills for beef cattle grazing. It passes a former horse-racing track, crosses a picturesque tributary of the Kawakawa River, across a small bridge, and then a road crossing before pulling into Taumarere Station.

Opposite: A diesel locomotive is used when 'Gabriel' is in the workshop.

Below: The train travels down the main street of Kawakawa much to the delight of passengers and the locals.

THE *NORTHERN EXPLORER*: AUCKLAND TO WELLINGTON

PORT TO PORT

This is a journey that showcases the New Zealand countryside and its varied, stunning and dynamic scenery. The *Northern Explorer*, occasionally called 'Dora the Explorer' (and up until 2012, the *Overlander*) travels along the North Island main trunk line between the capital, Wellington, and its largest city, Auckland (and vice versa); two of New Zealand's most beautiful and important ports.

This epic 681-km (423-mile) trip operated by KiwiRail Scenic Journeys (a division of KiwiRail) departs from the historic Wellington Railway Station on Bunny Street within walking distance of the picturesque Wellington Harbour and the Cook Strait Ferry Terminal. There are many ways to admire the harbour including walking around parts of it in the downtown area or riding the Wellington Cable Car from Lambton Quay to the Botanic Garden perched on the summit 120 m (394 ft) above for uninterrupted views of the city and the harbour below. This funicular railway operates on a 1,000 mm (3 foot 3⅜ inch) track over a distance of 628 m (2,060 ft).

The day-long *Northern Explorer* railway journey to Auckland enables travellers to take in a variety of New Zealand landscapes within the comfort of air-conditioned carriages and from panoramic windows (non-reflective and non-tinted) that extend well beyond the sides to partially across the roof. In addition to taking in views of both Wellington and Auckland Harbours, passengers can admire coastal stretches, lush agricultural pastures, pristine forests, glacial-fed rivers, snow-capped volcanic domes within Tongariro National Park and some masterful railway engineering feats.

Trains depart from platform 9 of Wellington Station on Tuesdays, Fridays and Sundays (departing at 7.55 a.m., arriving 6.45 p.m.) and Auckland on Mondays, Thursdays and Saturdays (departing at 7.45 a.m., arriving at 6.20 p.m.). Passengers need to check in at least 20 minutes before departure to be allocated seating and the queue can be long. Those with bags to check into the luggage van need to allocate extra time.

THE TRAIN

Overnight train services were initially hauled by steam locomotives before diesels were used. Trains are now hauled by a single DFB class locomotive of 2,400 horsepower. Its carriage configuration is one AKC class, three AK class, one AKL luggage van and an AKV

power/viewing van situated at the rear when it travels south to north but at the front when it is going from north to south (its open sides are perfect for photography). Advanced air-bag suspension in the carriages ensures a smoother and quieter ride.

Passengers can check large bags into the luggage car but smaller bags can be carried onto the train and stored in racks above the seat. There is limited space for bicycles and surfboards. Wheelchair access is available but only two wheelchair passengers can be accommodated on any journey.

Trains are fully licensed to serve alcohol and passengers are not allowed to consume their own alcohol onboard. A superb range of food and cool beverages are served including local beers and wines. There is a GPS-triggered route commentary in two

languages in all seats where passengers can listen, via headphones, to a detailed description of each destination that the train passes.

THE JOURNEY

When the *Northern Explorer* was introduced in 2012, several stops along the way were eliminated to shorten the journey. Stops are now made at Paraparaumu, Palmerston North, Ohakune, National Park, Otorohanga (for Waitamo), Hamilton and Papakura.

Within minutes of leaving Wellington Railway Station and skirting a section of the harbour, the train heads north via two long tunnels emerging minutes later near Glenside. The immediate change in scenery is dramatic as much of this part of Wellington is forested before urbanization takes over again on its journey into Porirua located on the shores of a sheltered inlet of the Tasman

Sea. The train travels along the eastern shore of the inlet with the morning sun creating a perfect mirror image of the low hills and yachts moored on the tranquil waterway.

The train rattles across a bridge near Ivey Bay with Porirua Harbour seen on the right-hand side. Within minutes, it reaches the coastline parallel to the busy State Highway 1 lined with peak-hour traffic and inches its way into the capital. This is one of the most picturesque sections of the journey with dazzling views of the Tasman Sea and the rugged coastline near the village of Paekakariki.

Kapiti Island (delicious Kapiti ice creams, made elsewhere in New Zealand, are served on the train) is clearly visible and despite once supporting a thriving whale oil industry, the island now plays a vital role in the preservation of native New Zealand birds as it is a bird sanctuary. A successful eradication programme has eliminated introduced predator pests and the birds thrive in their protected environment.

The train climbs though the Tararua Ranges created through the geological uplifting that also created the Southern Alps. This range now forms the backbone to the North Island.

There is a change of drivers at Palmerston North, and later at National Park and Hamilton. Photographers will be pleased to note that many drivers will slow the train down below the normal operating speed as it passes unique features of the landscape such as scenic rivers and iconic viaducts.

Just prior to Palmerston North (Palmerston or Palmy to the locals and not to be confused with Palmerston on the South Island), the train crosses the Manawatu River, one of many New Zealand rivers that is especially popular for white-water rafting.

After Taihape the train passes through Waiouru Station, which, at 814 m (2,671 ft) above sea level, is the highest train station in New Zealand. Beyond the town, the train crosses the Tangiwai Bridge over the Whangaehu River.

It passes through the small town of Ohakune, then crosses the spectacular Hapuawhenua Viaduct within Tongariro National Park. The original viaduct of 284 m (932 ft) is supported by 13 concrete piers and four steel towers and is 45 m (148 ft) above the valley below with its almost indiscernible stream. This viaduct became redundant in 1987 when a new concrete viaduct was constructed, however, it is still possible for adventurers to walk across and admire the old structure.

The snow-capped volcanic peaks of Tongariro, Ngauruhoe and Ruapehu within Tongariro National Park are seen well before the train arrives in the park. Just after leaving the national park

the train travels down the engineering feat known as the Raurimu Spiral, which was built in 1898 to enable trains to negotiate the steep incline between the Whanganui River Valley and the volcanic plateau above.

Mountains such as the North Island Volcanic Plateau presented a major obstacle to steam train travel in days gone by and the Raurimu Spiral overcame the problem of a rapid rise in altitude over a short distance. Using a route where the train loops back on itself and spirals around using tunnels and bridges, trains are able to rise 149 m (456 ft) at a gradient of 1:52 over a distance of some 7 km (4⅓ miles).

Otorohanga is the next stop and destination for passengers wishing to explore Waitamo Glowworm Caves. These limestone caves are home to a range of passive and activity adventures including caving or boating through the caves to admire the luminescent glowworms.

In the late afternoon, the train arrives into Hamilton, New Zealand's fourth largest city with a population of 162,000 people. It is a student town with a sizeable number of people having an association with Waikato University, named after the river that

flows through the city. More and more residents are commuters working in Auckland and regular train services ensure they arrive as quickly and safely as possible.

The *Northern Explorer* finally arrives into Auckland Strand Station at Ngaohe Place near the city centre and the Britomart Transport Centre. New Zealand's largest city is the leading international gateway and is known as the 'City of Sails' because of the numerous yachts moored around its expansive and picturesque harbour.

What is one the world's most beautiful harbours is best seen from the 220 m (722 ft) high observation deck of Sky Tower located within SkyCity Auckland in the centre of the downtown area.

Above: Most train drivers slow down at important sights so that photographers can capture the spectacular scenery.

Opposite: Sections of the Rangitikei River crossed on the journey were used as backdrops in the movie *The Lord of the Rings: The Fellowship Ring*.

Page 131: Ride the Wellington Cable Car from the harbour to the Botanic Gardens for panoramic harbour views.

WELLINGTON TO WAIRARAPA

PORT TO PINOT

Wairarapa is one hour from Wellington, the New Zealand capital. It is accessible by a daily train, perfect for a day or weekend visit, which leaves Wellington Railway Station near Wellington Harbour and travels north-east through the valley terminating in Masterton, the region's largest town. The service provides access to the Wairarapa townships of Featherston, Martinborough (via a connecting shuttle at Featherston), Greytown (via a connecting shuttle at Woodside), Carterton and Masterton.

The Wairarapa is a region of spectacular coastlines wide valleys and quaint colonial townships. Despite being a rural retreat it also offers a sophisticated lifestyle as it is home to vineyards, restaurants, olive groves and rolling pastures where sheep, beef and dairy cattle happily graze. While the vines were first planted near Masterton in 1883, the region is now home to wineries in Martinborough, Gladstone and Masterton. Martinborough is popular with those who enjoy Pinot Noir, a variety which put the town on the world stage. There are 20 wineries located within close proximity to each other making it unique in New Zealand.

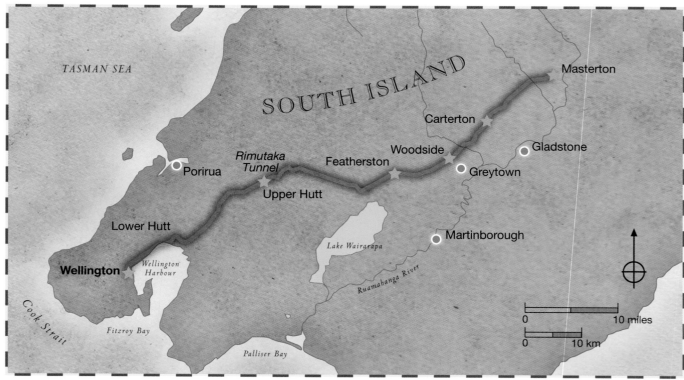

Gladstone, further north, is also recognised for producing stunning wines. Masterton's vineyards are primarily located in Opaki, including Paper Road Vineyard, which five times a year welcomes historic steam trains that travel from Steam Incorporated's Paekakariki base, north of Wellington.

The colonial village of Greytown is New Zealand's first planned inland town and was once the region's fruit bowl. These days, there are few orchards but its distinctive character has made it a desirable place to live.

A rail route over the Rimutaka Range was chosen in the early 1870s but the grade on the other side of the Pukuratahi Valley was too steep for normal trains and required one like the Fell (see p. 136). The line over the range opened in 1878 and reached

Masterton in 1880 then, in 1897, it connected to Woodville and the Napier to Palmerston North Line.

Transdev Wellington operates passenger services named the Wairarapa Connection between Wellington and Masterton via the Rimutaka Tunnel five times daily from Monday to Thursday, six on Friday and twice daily every Saturday, Sunday and public holiday. Excursion trains also use the tunnel, such as railway-enthusiast specials and trains to the Toast Martinborough Festival.

Above: Passengers will enjoy the scenic landscape including the Pakuratahi River.

Opposite: The Wairarapa Connection pulling into Featherston Station.

THE TRAIN

The train of six carriages that travels through the Wairarapa is hauled by a diesel locomotive that operates on the Metlink Greater Wellington network. Carriages are modern, light and open with panoramic windows and adjustable curtains. The seating arrangement is two seats on either side of the aisle. At the back of each seat there is a dropdown table and power points are located beneath seats for those who need to power up communications devices. Passengers can take bikes onto the train (bike storage racks are also located at stations). Audio announcements are made as the trains approach stations and there is also a digital read-out.

THE JOURNEY

Trains depart from Wellington Railway Station situated on Bunny Street. Wellington, wrapped around the harbour on the North Island's southern tip, isn't New Zealand's biggest city but it is the capital.

During morning rush hours, platforms are crowded with commuters arriving for their working day (some 30,000 daily). Passengers travelling to Wairarapa are free to choose their seating with the right-hand side being in the morning sunlight. Some 2,000 commuters use the Wairarapa service on average working days.

FELL LOCOMOTIVE MUSEUM, FEATHERSTON

The Featherston Fell Locomotive Museum is home to the fully-restored Fell locomotive H199; the only one of its type in the world. This loco was originally called Mont Cenis after the pass of the same name between Italy and France where the original Fell train operated. Developed in 1863, the engine incorporated John Fell's simple friction drive system where smooth, horizontally powered locomotive wheels were held against a raised centre rail. There is also a Fell brake-van F210 plus photos of Rimutaka Incline (from Cross Creek to Summit); New Zealand's steepest railway from 1878 to 1955. The locomotive, built in 1875, spent its entire time on the incline which climbed 265 m (869 ft) in 1.8 km (just over one mile). The 8.8-km (5½-mile) long Rimutaka Tunnel built in 1955 made the engines redundant. Some eight years and 9,000 volunteer hours were devoted to the restoration.

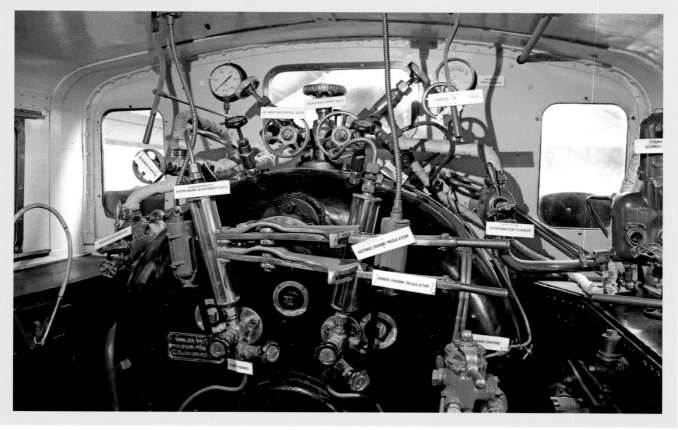

Within minutes of departing, the train passes the Westpac Stadium, home to the Hurricanes rugby team. It then edges around the spectacular harbour foreshore and runs adjacent to a freeway.

While the train stops at stations like Petone and Waterloo, being an express it bypasses suburban stations like Ava, Woburn, Wingate and Taita. The view becomes more rural by the time the train arrives in Manor Park with its verdant golf course.

After 40 minutes, the train stops at Upper Hutt Station with distant forested hills on the right. It enters the first significant tunnel, then emerges into a forested and agricultural landscape that is dramatically different from the suburbia at the tunnel's entrance. Not long afterwards, the train passes through the Rimutaka Tunnel of 8.8 km (5½ miles); New Zealand's second longest tunnel for scheduled passenger trains.

In the Wairarapa region, each town has its own unique character and appeals to different people for different reasons.

FEATHERSTON

From Wellington, Featherston is the first of the Wairarapa villages at which the train stops. This is the best gateway for the coastline of Cape Palliser and Martinborough. Featherston itself is a vibrant country town selling local cheeses, olive oil and cured meats. Of particular interest in town is the Fell Locomotive Museum (see opposite).

MARTINBOROUGH

Even though Martinborough has long been a service town for the South Wairarapa, in 1980 a government study indicated the soil and climate had potential for vineyards, and the area was transformed into a premium wine-producing region. There are now over 20 boutique vineyards within walking or cycling distance of the town square, which is laid out like a Union Jack. Most wineries provide tasting experiences for Sauvignon Blanc, Riesling, Pinot Gris and Pinot Noir varieties. Some have restaurants to satisfy the cravings of visitors including hungry bikers who cycle short distances between wineries. Ata Rangi, Poppies, Palliser Estate and Margrain are popular wineries while Martinborough Brewery adds a different dimension. There is a variety of accommodation including the stately Martinborough Hotel built in 1882, which holds court in the square, while neighbouring colonial buildings house innovative restaurants, homeware stores and gift shops.

GREYTOWN

Passengers visiting Greytown need to get off at Woodside Station, 5 km (3 miles) to the west of the town. Greytown is a sophisticated Victorian country village with antique stores, fashion boutiques, interior design outlets, cafés and restaurants lining the main street. Many are housed within restored wooden buildings with Cobblestones Early Settlers Museum located next to the acclaimed Schoc Chocolate shop. The White Swan is a gracious boutique country hotel with uniquely decorated rooms.

CARTERTON

An artistic community based here ensures the town is best known for its country creativity. Attractions in town include Paua World (crafted abalone or paua shell as it is known locally) and Stonehenge Aotearoa (based on Stonehenge). Carterton is also the gateway to Gladstone's wineries.

MASTERTON

Masterton, Wairarapa's largest town, is family-friendly and includes Queen Elizabeth Park which has a flying fox, paddle boats, mini-golf, bike hire and a miniature steam train. The neighbouring Wool Shed offers visitors a realistic look into New Zealand's pioneering history by tracing sheep farming and shearing. Nearby, Hood Aerodrome houses a rare collection of First World War aircraft. The Wairarapa is also home to nine golf courses and is where Sir Bob Charles, one of New Zealand's golfing legends, honed his skills.

Above: The diesel locomotive of the Wairarapa Connection joining the carriages at Wellington Station.

GLENBROOK VINTAGE RAILWAY

A WORKING MUSEUM

The train network of the Glenbrook Vintage Railway (GVR) is built and operated by volunteers in an effort to keep New Zealand's railway heritage alive. It operates from Glenbrook to Victoria Avenue in Waiuku, which are small towns situated due south of Auckland and approximately 45 minutes drive from Auckland International Airport.

Glenbrook is located on a railway line that continues east to join the main north–south KiwiRail network near Pukekohe. It was once part of the New Zealand Railways (NZR) Waiuku branch line, which existed from 1922 until it closed in 1967. Members of the Railway Enthusiasts Society began building the GVR in 1970 and in 1977, a steam-hauled service between Glenbrook and Pukeoware commenced. In 1986, an extension to Fernleigh was completed and then a further extension to Victoria Avenue was opened in 2010. There are plans to extend the line by some

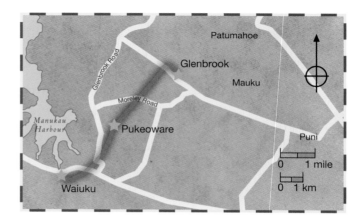

500 m (547 yards) to its ultimate terminus at Tamakae Reserve in Waiuku on Manukau Harbour. Glenbrook Railway Station is located just to the east of the small township of Glenbrook.

Above: A diesel-hauled train approaching Glenbrook Station.

Left: The fireman shovelling coal into the firebox of the boiler.

Opposite: Train driver keeping a careful eye on the dials of a steam train.

Volunteers who staff the railway all wear period railway uniforms to add to the authenticity and nostalgia of what has become a working museum.

Train services operate every Sunday and most public holidays from late October to early June while the train is available for charter all year-round. Trains depart from Glenbrook at 11.00 a.m., 12.30 p.m., 2.00 p.m. and 3.30 p.m. Return trains depart from Victoria Avenue at 11.30 a.m., 1.00 p.m., 2.30 p.m. and 4.00 p.m.

Special days and events are held: the 'Day Out with Thomas' is especially popular with children as one of the trains is decked out as 'Thomas the Tank Engine'. The GVR uses a Bagnall 2475 steam locomotive for these days.

While not staged as regularly, Steam and Vintage Festivals are also held at the station every four years or so with the last one being in February 2017. At these times Glenbrook Station becomes a focus for steam engines of all types from trains to boats and miniature locomotives, and cars to static machinery during the day-long gathering.

THE TRAIN

The journey to Glenbrook offers the opportunity to experience a self-contained steam railway. Various steam and diesel locomotives are used by the railway, with steam locomotives such as Ww 644, a 4-6-4 tank, and Ja 1250, a 4-8-2 tender locomotive, the ones most commonly used. Both were built at Hillside Workshops in Dunedin; Ww 644 in 1915 and Ja 1250 in 1949.

There are currently five steam locomotives and five vintage diesel locomotives in the GVR stable with the diesels mostly employed for way and works (track and infrastructure maintenance). First-class comfort is offered in the Parlour Car, which is a recent addition to the carriage configuration. Complimentary tea, coffee, juices, soft drinks and cakes are served in this car only on both legs of the journey.

An open wagon is also used and is the best location for obtaining photos, although the stops at Waiuku and the workshop at Pukeoware also present excellent photo opportunities as passengers are able to alight from the train.

More than a dozen ex-NZR carriages and a selection of historic goods vehicles are also used or housed at the GVR workshop. These include an 1879 six-wheeled car to more recent carriages of the early 20th century, all featuring varnished wood panelling.

THE JOURNEY

Passengers gather at Glenbrook Station to buy tickets, enjoy refreshments and browse the souvenir and bookshop prior to the departure of the trains. There are actually two 'A' type station buildings; one is the original Glenbrook Station building and the other relocated from Patumahoe Station just east of Glenbrook.

Nearby, the caretaker's house is a 1922 railway house, which was relocated from Waiuku to Glenbrook Station in 1995. Glenbrook's current signal box was relocated from yards near Gladstone Road in Auckland. This Auckland 'B' signal box has been fully restored and is classified as a heritage building having won an award in the process.

The train covers a total distance of 15 km (9⅓ miles) with the return journey taking just over one hour. The landscape along the way is typically rural with low rolling hills devoted to agriculture especially pasture land for beef cattle. This is punctuated with stands of trees especially pines. Trains depart from Glenbrook Station to the terminus at Victoria Avenue Station in Waiuku, where passengers can alight to explore the heritage town and return on a later train.

Located on the southern reaches of the Waiuku River, which flows into Manukau Harbour, Waiuku is a rural service town. The Kentish Hotel, dating back to 1851 when it opened as an inn, is one of New Zealand's oldest pubs. Other heritage buildings in the town include Waiuku Gaol, The Creamery, Hartmann House and Pollock Cottage. There is a museum and folk village plus a heritage trail, which includes the Wesley Methodist Church for panoramic town views.

On the return journey, the train stops for 15 minutes for passengers to alight and inspect the railway workshop at Pukeoware. This workshop is not only responsible for maintaining and restoring GVR rolling stock but also that of other railways in the country on a contract basis.

Visitors can also opt to enjoy a four-kilometre (2½-mile) motor jigger ride from Glenbrook Station to Morley Road that leaves just after the train has departed. Motor jiggers are small, petrol-powered vehicles that run on the rails and are used to transport maintenance workers along the railway. At the location of the work, it can be removed from the rails to allow trains to pass. The jiggers can take two, four or six people. Hand jigger rides are also possible within the yards of Glenbrook Station.

Left: Ww 644 steam locomotive.

Opposite: The train makes a scheduled stop at the Pukeoware workshop for passengers to inspect the society's ongoing projects.

THE SOUTH ISLAND

INTRODUCTION

In 1862, New Zealand's first recognized railway opened as a privately-owned, horse-drawn 'tramline' used to carry extracted chromite from Dun Mountain 21.5 km (13 miles) south-east of Nelson at the northern tip of the South Island. While originally for the transportation of ore, freight and passengers were also carried with the latter between the town and the port. A horse-drawn tram was used (it was also called a bus) to transport passengers and the service remained viable until it was closed in 1901.

The first steam-powered public railway on the South Island dates back to 1863 with the commissioning of the Christchurch to Ferrymead line to the south-east of Christchurch on the banks of the Heathcote River. Goods unloaded from ships in Port Lyttleton were transported here and then into Christchurch. It's possible to visit Ferrymead Heritage Park for vintage steam train and tram rides.

In 1867 a 2.6-km (1½-mile) tunnel was dug through the Port Hills to provide access from Port Lyttleton to Christchurch. In the Southland, a 12-km (7¾-mile) long wooden rail line was opened in 1864 between Invercargill and Makarewa.

Dunedin Railways operates scheduled and charter services, such as the Taieri Gorge Railway and *The Seasider*, as well as linking Queenstown and Wanaka via a train and road coach combination.

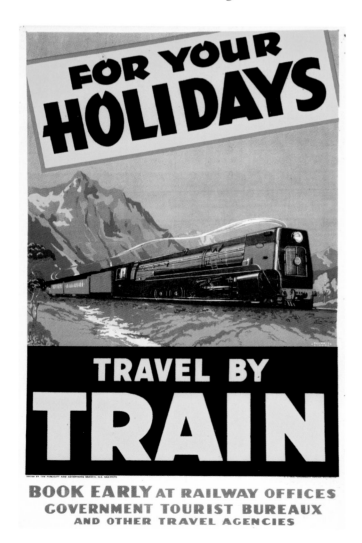

They also operate occasional services to Christchurch and then on to Hokatika on the west coast. Trains of the Dunedin Railways are also available for charter journeys.

Pleasant Point Museum and Railway is unique as it is where train buffs will be able to see and ride on the world's only Model T Ford Railcar RM 4. The vehicle on display is a rebuild of the original RM 4 of 1925, which operated from 1926 to 1931 on the Edendale to Wyndham Railway line situated in the Southland. It is based on a modified Model T Ford one ton (tonne) truck chassis and running gear.

Weka Pass Railway is a rural railway that operates vintage steam and diesel-electric locomotives along a 13-km (8-mile) track through the Weka Pass on the outskirts of Waipara 60 km (37 miles) north of Christchurch. The original line opened to Waikari in 1882 and then northwards to Waiau in 1919. Regular passenger services were withdrawn in 1939 but volunteers conduct a tourist train service on a section of the line on the first and third Sunday of every month and on most public holidays. On most occasions the train is hauled by a 1909 A class 'Pacific' steam locomotive, the only one of its type still in operation.

Some of the great railway journeys of the world can be experienced on New Zealand's South Island including the *TranzAlpine* (see page 144) and the Taieri Gorge Railway (see page 152). Sadly, the *Coastal Pacific* from Picton to Christchurch was badly damaged in an earthquake in 2016 resulting in its cancellation for many months.

Below: The *TranzAlpine* crosses the Southern Alps through some of New Zealand's most scenic landscapes.

Opposite left: Old railway poster.

THE *TRANZALPINE*: CHRISTCHURCH TO GREYMOUTH

SCENIC JOURNEY ACROSS THE SOUTHERN ALPS

The *TranzAlpine* is considered by many to be the most picturesque rail journey in New Zealand and rated as one of the best in the world. It was gold that spurred an interest in charting an alpine route across the Southern Alps of the South Island and now it is the *TranzAlpine* tourist train that brings additional wealth to the region.

Gold was discovered in Greymouth on the west coast in 1864 and a rudimentary road was completed in 1866 to enable those seeking their fortune to cross the Southern Alps from Christchurch.

Railways were introduced to Christchurch in its early history with the first steam-powered railway being the Christchurch to Ferrymead line commissioned in 1863.

The portion of the Main South Line on which the *TranzAlpine* runs was opened from Christchurch to Rolleston in 1866. The easternmost portion from Rolleston to Darfield was opened by the Canterbury Provincial Government in 1874 and the Greymouth to Brunner section in 1876. These two lines were united into one in 1923 and included the impressive 8.5-km (5⅓-mile) long Otira Tunnel whose construction commenced in 1908. The route passes through 16 other tunnels and traverses four viaducts.

Trains known as the Christchurch to Greymouth Express serviced the line until 1987 when the New Zealand Railways Corporation replaced them with the *TranzAlpine*. The express trains once included 'Grass Grub' carriages of converted 88-seater railcars and named after their green livery.

The current daily schedule (it operates daily except on Christmas Day) has an 8.15 a.m. departure from Christchurch, 1.05 p.m. arrival in Greymouth, 2.05 p.m. departure from Greymouth and a 6.31 p.m. arrival back into Christchurch.

THE TRAIN
Passengers on the *TranzAlpine* can book large bags into the luggage car as there is limited space within the carriages above each seat. Seats are allocated upon arrival at the station and are mostly facing in the direction of travel although there are some four-seat spaces with a table between. Panoramic windows (non-tinted and non-reflective for better photography) and skylights are a feature of the one-class, AK carriages made in Dunedin and introduced on the service in 2011. The bogies on the passenger cars of the current train have secondary suspension in the form of airbags which, in addition to the primary steel and rubber spring suspension, provide a superior ride.

Passengers can listen to a commentary of the journey via in-seat headsets and there's a kids' pack to keep them entertained. The café serves light meals and beverages, such as local beers and wines, to be taken back for in-seat consumption. An observation car completes the facilities.

THE JOURNEY
The *TranzAlpine* heads west from Christchurch and stops at Rolleston, Darfield, Springfield, Arthur's Pass, Otira and Moana before reaching Greymouth on the Tasman Sea, a journey of 224 km (139 miles) that takes about five hours.

Above: The train travelling through stunning scenery alongside the Waimakariri River, one of the largest of the north Canterbury rivers in the South Island.

Opposite: The *TranzAlpine* in winter travelling through Cass Bank, in the Canterbury Region of the South Island, with its impressive alpine backdrop near Lake Sarah.

Following pages: The *TranzAlpine* crossing the Waimakariri Bridge over the river of the same name.

Christchurch is New Zealand's second largest city of over 400,000 (with the satellite towns from Rangiora to Rolleston included). Known as the Garden City, the 30-ha (74-acre) parklands of Hagley Park and Christchurch Botanic Gardens adjoin the city centre and are dissected by the gently meandering Avon River. Settled in the 1850s, Christchurch is a planned city with a central city square that makes it very British in appearance. Its Gothic Revival heritage architecture is best seen in buildings such as Canterbury College (now the University of Christchurch), Canterbury Museum and the famous Christ Church Cathedral (mostly still intact after the disastrous 2011 earthquake which resulted in the collapse of the church spire).

The train departs from Christchurch Railway Station in Addington close to the city centre. Suburban Christchurch quickly passes giving way at Rolleston to the agricultural lands of the Canterbury Plains. From here, the tracks cross alluvial plains between Rolleston and Springfield at the base of the Southern Alps. Local train enthusiasts call this section of track to Arthur's Pass 'KB Country' as it was famous for the use of KB class steam

locomotives from 1939 to 1968 (the K class prototype was introduced in the North Island in 1932). Wide, glacier-fed rivers dissect the plains dropping rocky moraine in their wake and this is most obvious from panoramic windows or the open-sided observation car as the train skirts the southern floodplain of the wide, braided Waimakariri River.

The train continues along this and Broken River before crossing a bridge over the Waimakariri River. From here the train starts to ascend the Southern Alps towards Arthur's Pass at an altitude of 740 m (2,425 ft). At 73 m (240 ft) high the Staircase Viaduct is one of the most impressive on the entire journey.

While the train only stops for five minutes, there is time to photograph the surrounding snow-capped peaks and stretch the legs at Arthur's Pass, one of several gateways for enjoying the many recreational activities in the Southern Alps. Located 153 km (95 miles) west of Christchurch, this small alpine town was named after Sir Arthur Dudley Dobson who, in the mid 19th century, was tasked with identifying a suitable passage across the Southern Alps. This section of the alps is protected by the Department of

Conservation within the Arthur's Pass National Park, which is covered in forests punctuated by steep snow-covered peaks.

Back on board, the alpine scenery is lost for a short while as the train passes through the Otira Tunnel, at 8.5 km (5⅓ miles), one of the longest railway tunnels in New Zealand.

West Coast topography and vegetation on the descent from the Southern Alps are in marked contrast to the ascent to Arthur's Pass. Lush temperate rainforest thrives in the isolated wet coastal slopes and river valleys, and remain mostly intact as the original settlers didn't clear them since the land was unsuitable for agriculture. This is great new news for adventurous visitors as there are many opportunities for ecotourism and recreation.

More accessible native forests were logged extensively along the route of the Midland Railway from Stillwater to Jacksons once it opened in 1895. Every station and siding on that section of the route had a sawmill nearby and most had bush tramways to bring out the logs. The largest was the 22-km (13½-mile) Lake Brunner Sawmilling Company Tramway that connected to the main line at Ruru. Much of the forest has been protected since 1999 as conservation land. Some 24 per cent of New Zealand is covered in native forests with the dominant type along the railway being temperate rainforest known as lowland podocarp that includes tree species such as kahikatea, totara, rimu, matai and miro.

Beech forests are located at higher altitudes and most commonly in the northern parts of Westland although they do stretch to the far south. Southern or Antarctic beech forests (Nothofagus or Fuscospora genus) are important to the scientific community as they are climatic indicators. Fossil evidence suggests that they once grew on Antarctica when it was much warmer and wetter. Antarctica was then part of the ancient supercontinent of the southern hemisphere known as Gondwana with related beech species now found in southern South America, southern Africa, eastern Australia including Tasmania and New Caledonia as well as New Zealand.

Greymouth rail terminus is located near Mawhera Quay on the southern side of the Grey River. With a population of just 12,000 'Coasters' (as the locals are known), it is the largest town on the whole of the sparsely populated West Coast of the South Island. Named after a prominent New Zealand politician, the district was settled by Europeans from the 1860s onwards after gold was discovered. While a brisk walk from the train terminus, the History House Museum is worth visiting as it chronicles the district's past and its association with mining. There is also an old steam train to admire at Shantytown about 12 km (7½ miles) south of the town. Greymouth is also known for its pounamu, a type of carved greenstone or jade as well as being the home of Monteith's Brewing Company.

THE SEASIDER: OAMARU TO DUNEDIN

SPECTACULAR COASTAL SCENERY

The Pacific Coast Railway north of Dunedin was considered one of the highlights of a now bygone South Island Main Trunk Line journey that passed along the East Coast of New Zealand's South Island. The current tourist train replicates part of the journey on comfortable Dunedin Silver Fern carriages with panoramic windows, air conditioning and table service.

The Dunedin to Palmerston railway line was completed in 1879 but it wasn't until 1945 that the Bluff (far south) to Picton (far north) line was completed. The track is now owned by OnTrack, a state-owned New Zealand Government enterprise.

In 2004, *The Seasider* started services between Dunedin and Palmerston and, in doing so, became the only passenger train service on the South Island Main Trunk Line south of Rolleston after *The Southerner*, operated by Tranzrail ceased services in 2002 (The *TranzAlpine* and the *Coastal Pacific* operate further north on the island). In 2015, some services were extended to include regular journeys to Oamaru via Moeraki Boulders.

Various journeys are operated by Dunedin Railways including Dunedin to Waitati and return (90 minutes), Dunedin to Moeraki Boulders and return (seven hours), and Dunedin to Oamaru and return (seven hours). From November to May, *The Waitati Seasider* operates a frequent schedule over a distance of 25 km (15½ miles).

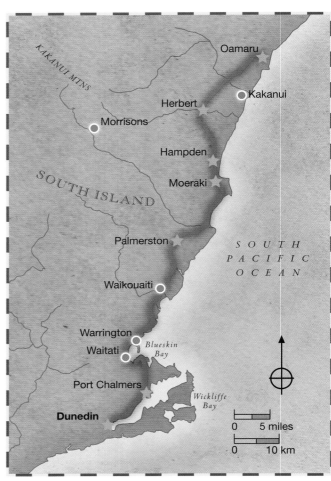

The Dunedin to Oamaru and Moeraki Boulders trains operate from 9.30 a.m. and return at 4.30 p.m. from May to September and on selected days at other times of the year.

THE TRAIN

The two-car, Dunedin Silver Fern RM24 railcar is comfortably appointed and finished with wood veneer panelling. On the forward journey, the preferred seating is on the right-hand side of the journey in seats numbered A and B, although passengers can move about, especially if the train isn't crowded. The driver sits in a compartment of the front car, which was built by Nissho Iwai in 1972 for New Zealand Railways. The train can carry up to 94 passengers and travels at a maximum speed of 120 km/h (75 mph).

It offers an all-weather trip as the carriages are enclosed and heated in cooler months while small open-air sections between carriages enable passengers to better experience the countryside in warmer times. Light snacks (track snacks) and beverages are served onboard, and the train is fully licensed to serve alcohol.

THE JOURNEY

Like its sister train, the Taieri Gorge Railway (see page 152), the journey on *The Seasider* sets off from Dunedin Railway Station. Passengers on all services enjoy views of Otago Harbour, Port Chalmers, Careys Bay, Mapoutahi Peninsula and Blueskin Bay. Trip highlights are listed in a brochure available from the ticket office. It needs noting that occasional coastal fog can affect the enjoyment of this journey.

Within seconds of departing Dunedin Station, the train travels on a track that runs along the foreshore of Otago Harbour with its little fishing bays and yacht moorings. The Dunedin to Port Chalmers line was the first to be built to the New Zealand standard gauge, 1,067 mm (3 foot 6 inch).

Port Chalmers is the port for Otago and where European settlers first arrived in 1848. It was then, and still is, Dunedin's freight link to the outside world as well as now being a popular port-of-call for cruise ships. Miners and entrepreneurs arrived in Dunedin via the port and this is how the settlement flourished to become, in its day, New Zealand's commercial centre.

As the train slowly climbs several hills and passes through tunnels beyond the harbour, the landscape becomes mostly forests interspersed with agricultural land.

There is a pause in the township of Waitati beside Blueskin Bay before the train returns to Dunedin.

Another service extends beyond Waitati all the way north to Oamaru taking in Palmerston, Moeraki Boulders and Herbert plus a few other coastal destinations. Big ocean views are the highlight of the seven-hour return journey on what is the *Oamaru Seasider*. Beaches such as Warrington, Karitane and Katiki are passed along the way and there is a one-hour stop in Oamaru to explore the whitestone buildings of the town's Victorian architecture precinct. Other attractions of interest in the coastal town include quirky Steampunk sculptures, art galleries, cafés and craft shops.

A hop-on, hop-off option on this train journey is the *Moeraki Boulders Seasider* where passengers can alight from the *Oamaru Seasider* to admire the spectacular Moeraki Boulders. Passengers who take this option have two hours to explore these geological phenomena and stroll along the beach before rejoining the train on its way back from Oamaru to Dunedin.

Above: When cruise ships are in port a special train meets passengers for a journey on the Taieri Gorge Railway.

Opposite: The *Oamaru Seasider* passing through its namesake town.

TAIERI GORGE RAILWAY

ONE OF THE WORLD'S GREAT TRAIN TRIPS

This journey on New Zealand's South Island is rated as one of the world's great train trips. Its appeal is partly the variety of landscapes the train passes through in a relatively short period of time and partly the triumph of the engineering to construct the track. In four hours the train from Dunedin to Pukerangi passes through urban Dunedin, across the lush farming land of the Taieri Plain, through the Maungatua Hills, down Mullocky Gully and then through the rugged gorge of the Taieri River, west of Dunedin. The service operates on most days: there are two choices with the

Dunedin to Pukerangi journey being the shorter option to the full trip which operates all the way to Middlemarch on specific days.

Tunnels and towering viaducts were hand hewn through mostly steep, metamorphic rock (schist) on the 58-km (36-mile) route to Pukerangi and a further two hours or 77 km (48 miles) to Middlemarch and what is now the end of the line. The line once extended all the way (235 km/146 miles) to Alexandra and Cromwell in Central Otago but the section from Middlemarch was closed in the mid 1970s.

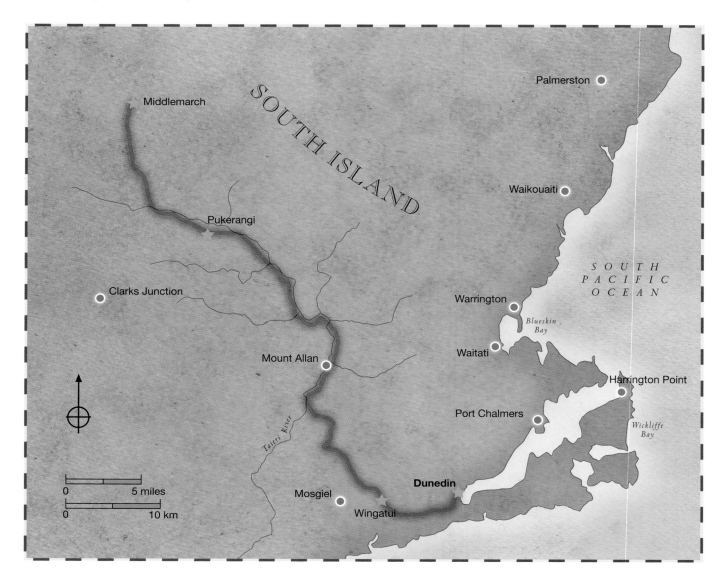

Above: Dunedin Railway Station, constructed from basalt rock, was once one of the busiest in New Zealand.

Various summer and winter schedules are available to Pukerangi but the Middlemarch extension in only available throughout the year on selected days. While most passengers buy a return ticket, single journey tickets are available. Dunedin is a busy cruise-ship port and a journey on the train is a popular shore excursion for many cruise passengers, so timetables are adjusted to accommodate them. Bookings are highly recommended for this popular journey especially during the warmer months from October to April. Cruise-ship business is important for the railway and most days when cruise ships are in port, the train journeys down to Port Chalmers and back to collect and drop off these passengers.

New Zealand Railways ran daily passengers services on this line until the mid 1970s. Originally steam trains, these were replaced by Vulcan Railcars until passenger numbers declined.

In 1990, the Central Otago line was closed after the completion of the Clyde hydroelectric power station. The Otago Excursion Train Trust operated passenger trains from 1979, then services operated by the Taieri Gorge Railway Limited commenced services that ran through the Taieri River Gorge. Had it not been for the Trust and the Dunedin City Council, this line would have closed. The Trust organised the 'Save the Train Appeal' to raise $1.2 million so they and the Dunedin Council could purchase the line from North Taieri to Middlemarch along with five DJ class diesel electric

locomotives. In 1995, the Trust and the Council established Taieri Gorge Railway Limited to operate train services from Dunedin Station. In 2014, Taieri Gorge Railway was rebranded as Dunedin Railways to reflect its diversity of destinations.

This railway owns more carriages on the South Island than New Zealand Rail and operates charter trips on the South Island including frequent trips on the South Island Main Trunk line or on the Midland line to the West Coast. It also operates *The Seasider* (see page 150).

THE TRAIN

Diesel locomotives (DJ class electric diesel built by Mitsubishi in 1960) haul at least half a dozen heritage carriages and two more modern air-conditioned carriages, one of which contains the snack car. Windows partially open in the heritage cars but not in the others.

Gradients of 1:50 are common on the journey and, as this is steep by railway standards, the locomotive takes the steeper inclines slowly but this works in everyone's favour as it makes for a steadier ride for photography.

The train has a liquor licence and beer, cider and wines may be purchased with iconic local Emerson's ales being available including the signature 'Taieri George' strong, smooth and spicy ale. This ale is named after George Emerson who was one of those instrumental in saving the line and also the father of the current brew master, Richard Emerson. Dunedin people proudly support their local brewer who has an impressive alehouse and restaurant in the town.

THE JOURNEY

Trains depart from Dunedin Railway Station although it's also possible to get on and off at Wingatui Station. Opened in 1906, Dunedin Station, known as the 'Gingerbread House', is considered to be the most photographed building in New Zealand. It was designed as the jewel in the New Zealand Railways' (NZR) crown in the city that was then the nation's commercial centre. Passengers on all Dunedin Railway services are advised to leave enough time to admire the sheer grandeur of the building with its rich, eccentric embellishments. Panels formed from some 725,760 porcelain tiles manufactured by Royal Doulton have been incorporated into the floor of the entrance lobby. These panels include a small steam engine, NZR's logo and other rail motifs. In 1994, the Dunedin Council purchased the station from the government for a nominal fee of one dollar.

During the journey there is a commentary by the train manager and there is also a complimentary illustrated guide to the route issued along with the tickets.

For the first 15 minutes, the train heads south down the South Island Main Trunk line to the turn-off point at Wingatui and the Central Otago branch line. It passes through the Caversham Tunnel, at 865 m (2,838 ft), the longest of 12 tunnels along the journey. At Wingatui, the train stops while the locomotive crew manually switch the train onto the branch line now owned by the City of Dunedin.

Agricultural activity is evident once out of the urban limits of Dunedin with dairy farms, orchards, horse studs and market gardens dominating. Further along the journey, extensive stands of commercial pine trees cover the hills.

Viaducts are a feature of the railway with the first and biggest structure on the journey being the Wingatui Viaduct, New Zealand's biggest wrought-iron structure and with a drop of 50 m (164 ft) to the gully below.

Excellent views of the river can be had from both sides of the train while photography is best done from the open platforms between each carriage. The Taieri is New Zealand's fourth longest river and brown trout can be caught here although river access is difficult. While tranquil on most occasions, flooding can turn it into a raging torrent with the 1980 flooding seeing 70 times the normal flow of water through the gorge.

At the farming hamlet of Pukerangi, the diesel locomotives are disconnected and relocated to the other end of the train for the return journey. The name means 'hills of heaven' and the countryside here is indeed a special and tranquil rural setting. While deserted now, Pukerangi was once a thriving community with its own school.

Passengers may disembark here to watch this process and to admire the rural countryside that lies at just 250 m (820 ft) above sea level. There is little else to do apart from watching the diesel being repositioned or watching cyclists unload their bikes from the luggage car in order to head off for the rail trail that begins at Middlemarch on the former railway line.

The complete journey to Middlemarch takes six hours with a one-hour stop at the end of the line. Middlemarch is the eastern portal for the popular Otago Central Rail Trail to which Dunedin Railways conveniently links.

Left: The train of the Taieri Gorge Railway snaking its way up through pine trees lining the gorge and beside the Taieri River.

RESOURCES

CONTACTS

Association of Tourist and Heritage Rail Australia Inc:
www.greatrailexperiencesaustralia.com.au
Australian Capital Tourism: www.tourism.act.gov.au
Destination NSW: www.destinationnsw.com.au
South Australia Tourism Commission:
www.visit-southaustralia.com.au
Tourism and Events Queensland: www.queensland.com
Tourism Northern Territory: www.tourismnt.com.au
Tourism Tasmania: www.tourismtasmania.com.au
Tourism Victoria: www.tourismvictoria.com.au
Tourism Western Australia: www.westernaustralia.com

RAILWAY WEBSITES, AUSTRALIA

AUSTRALIAN CAPITAL TERRITORY
Australian Railway Historical Society ACT Division:
www.arhsact.com.au

NEW SOUTH WALES
3801 Limited: www.3801limited.com.au
Australian Railway Historical Society NSW Division:
www.arhsnsw.com.au
Australian Railway Monument and Rail Journeys Museum:
railjny@nsw.chariot.net.au
Byron Bay Railway Company: www.byronbaytrain.com.au
Katoomba Scenic World: www.scenicworld.com.au
NSW TrainLink: www.nswtrainlink.com
Opal: www.opal.com.au
Transport Heritage NSW Ltd: www.heritageexpress.onfo
Yass Railway Heritage Centre: www.railway.yass.com.au
Zig Zag Railway: www.zigzagrailway.com.au

NORTHERN TERRITORY
The Ghan: www.greatsouthernrail.com.au

QUEENSLAND
Australian Railway Historical Society Queensland Division:
www.arhs-qld.org.au
G:link Gold Coast Light Rail: www.RideTheG.com.au
Kuranda Scenic Railway: www.ksr.com.au
Queensland Rail Travel: www.queenslandrailtravel.com.au
TRANSLink: www.translink.com.au

SOUTH AUSTRALIA
Cockle Train: www.steamranger.org.au
National Railway Museum Port Adelaide:
www.natrailmuseum.org.au
Pichi Richi Railway: www.pichirichirailway.org.au
Steamtown Heritage Rail Centre: www.steamtown.com.au
The Overland: www.greatsouthernrail.com.au

TASMANIA
Australian Railway Historical Society Tasmania Division:
www.railtasmania.com/arhs
Don River Railway: www.donriverrailway.com.au
Ida Bay Railway: www.idabayrailway.com.au
Launceston Tramway Museum:
www.launcestontramwaymuseum.org.au
Redwater Creek Steam and Heritage Society:
www.sheffieldsteam.com.au
Tasmanian Transport Museum: www.railtasmania.com/ttms
Wee Georgie Wood Railway: www.weegeorgiewood.com.au
West Coast Wilderness Railway: www.wcwr.com.au

VICTORIA
Australian Railway Historical Society Victorian Division:
www.arhsvic.com.au
Ballarat Tramway Museum: www.btm.org.au
Bellarine Railway: www.bellarinerailway.com.au
Metro Trains Melbourne: www.metrotrains.com.au
Mornington Railway: www.morningtonrailway.org.au
Puffing Billy Preservation Society: www.puffingbilly.com.au
Seymour Railway Heritage Centre: www.srhc.org.au

V/Line: www.vline.com.au
Victorian Goldfields Railway: www.vgr.com.au
Walhalla Goldfields Railway: www.walhallarail.com.au
Yarra Valley Railway: www.yvr.com.au

WESTERN AUSTRALIA

Hotham Valley Railway: www.hothamvalleyrailway.com.au
Indian Pacific: www.greatsouthernrail.com.au
Pemberton Tramway Company: www.pemtram.com.au
Rail Heritage Western Australia: www.railheritagewa.org.au
Transperth: www.transperth.wa.gov.au
Transwa: www.transwa.wa.gov.au

RAILWAY WEBSITES, NEW ZEALAND

Auckland's suburban trains www.mazz.co.nz
Bay of Islands Vintage Railway:
     www.bayofislandsvintagerailway.org.nz
Bush Tramway Club: www.bushtramwayclub.com
Dunedin Railways: www.dunedinrailways.co.nz
Fell Engine Museum: www.fellmuseum.org.nz
Ferrymead Heritage Park: www.ferrymead.org.nz
Glenbrook Vintage Railway: www.gvn.co.nz
KiwiRail: www.kiwirail.co.nz
KiwiRail Scenic Journeys: www.kiwirailscenic.co.nz
Metlink Wellington: www.metlink.org.nz
Taieri Gorge Railway: www.dunedinrailways.co.nz
The Seasider: www.dunedinrailways.co.nz
Tourism New Zealand: www.tourismnewzealand.com
Weka Pass Railway: www.wekapassrailway.co.nz
Wellington Cable Car: www.wellingtoncablecar.co.nz
Wellington's suburban trains www.transmetro.co.nz

GENERAL

Australian Rail Map: www.railmaps.com.au
The Man in Seat 61: www.seat61.com

READING

Bowden, David. 2015. *Enchanting Australia*. John Beaufoy
     Publishing.
Bryson, Bill. 2000. *Down Under*. Doubleday.
Kelly, Andrew and David Bowden. 1988. *Countries of the World,
     Australia*. Wayland.
Light, Liz. 2017. *Enchanting New Zealand*. John Beaufoy
     Publishing.
Solomon, Brian. 2011, *The World's Most Spectacular Railway
     Journeys*. John BeaufoyPublishing.
Solomon, Brian. 2015, *The World's Most Exotic Railway
     Journeys*. John BeaufoyPublishing.

ACKNOWLEDGEMENTS

Many people contributed valuable information and feedback in the preparation of this book. Particular thanks go to Selena Oh, Todd Rowling, George Stockton, Alan Reid, Shelley Winkle, Peter Steele (*Australind*), Bruce Smith and Melanie Reid (*Indian Pacific*), Paul Baker and Max Bullow (Hotham Valley Railway), Eric Jenkins and Matt Sullivan (Katoomba Scenic World), Jim Blake, Alfred Kua and Dana Urmonas (Glenelg Tram), Melanie Reid (*The Overland* and *The Ghan*), Lee Dixon (Don River Railway), Lisa Maclean, Greg Hallam, Becca Keegan, Marc Sleeman and Phil Bayne (Kuranda Scenic Railway), Maria Murnane (Melbourne to Ballarat), Chris Raggert, Alan Bailey and Nadine Hutchins (*Puffing Billy*), Jenny Na (Swan Hill Train), Barbara Smythe, Jeremy Browne and Maikha Ly (Pichi Richi Railway), Tan Siew Hoon (Sydney to Dubbo Train), Anne Leitch (Bay of Islands Vintage Railway), Toby Mann, Murray Bond, Barbara Reid, Lyall Kelpe (Taieri Gorge Railway and *The Seasider*), Ross Crook (Glenbrook Vintage Railway), Caitlin Madden, Kate Campbell and Lyna Hanis (Tourism New Zealand), Janet Tang and Simon Stichbury (*Northern Explorer*), Duncan Browne (*TranzAlpine*) and Katie Farman (Wairarapa).

ABOUT THE AUTHOR

David Bowden is a freelance photojournalist based in Malaysia who specializes in travel and the environment. While Australian, he's been in Asia for longer than he can remember and returns to his home country as an enthusiastic tourist. His love for train travel began when he journeyed daily to high school in Newcastle, New South Wales by steam train and he has since travelled on many of the great railways of the world. When he's not travelling he enjoys relaxing with his wife Maria and daughter Zoe. He is also the author of several titles in the *Enchanting* travel series, published by John Beaufoy Publishing.

INDEX

First published in the United Kingdom in 2017 by John Beaufoy Publishing,

11 Blenheim Court, 316 Woodstock Road, Oxford OX2 7NS, UK

www.johnbeaufoy.com

1 2 3 4 5 6 7 8 9 10

ISBN 978-1-909612-94-5

Designed by Glyn Bridgewater

Cartography by William Smuts

Project management by Rosemary Wilkinson

Printed and bound in Malaysia by Times Offset (M) Sdn. Bhd.

PHOTO CREDITS

All photos are by David Bowden with the exception of the following: Destination NSW (p.60, p. 79
top); The Don River Railway (pp. 114-115); Dunedin Railways (p.150, p. 154, p. 155); Great Southern
Rail (front cover, p. 19, p. 29 top, p. 117, p. 118, p. 119, p. 120, p. 121, p. 122, p. 123); Katoomba Scenic
World (p. 65); KiwiRail Scenic Journeys (back cover, p. 4, pp. 124-125, p. 133, p. 142, pp. 144-145,
p. 146, p. 147, p. 148, p. 149); Maikha Ly (front cover flap, pp. 2–3, p. 36); Paul Livingston, Capital
Country Tourism (p. 83 bottom); Pichi Richi Railway (p. 37); Puffing Billy (p. 47, p. 49); Queensland
Rail Travel (back cover flap, p. 87, p. 91, p. 96, pp. 100-101, p. 104); Skyrail Rainforest Cableway
(p. 105); Sovereign Hill (p. 52); Tourism and Events Queensland (p. 92, p. 94, p. 97); Tourism NT
(p. 116); Tourism Victoria (p. 55).

PACIFIC OCEAN

TASMAN SEA

Cape Rēinga
North Cape

Kaitaia
Kerikeri
28 Kawakawa
Whangarei
Dargaville

Great Barrier Island
Hauraki Gulf
Helensville
Coromandel
Auckland
Thames
31
Bay of Plenty
Hicks Bay
East Cape
Hamilton
Tauranga
Opotiki
Rotorua
Anaura Bay
Otorohanga
NORTH ISLAND
CENTRAL PLATEAU
Taupō
Gisborne
New Plymouth
Lake Taupō
Cape Egmont
29
Mt Ruapehu
Mahia Peninsula
Hawke's Bay
Napier
Hastings
Whanganui
Palmerston North
Masterton
Farewell Spit
Collingwood
Golden Bay
30 Greytown
Nelson
Picton
Cook Strait
Blenheim
Wellington
Cape Palliser

Cape Foulwind
Westport
Punakaiki
Kaikoura
Greymouth
SOUTH ISLAND
Hokitika
32
Waipara
Aoraki / Mt. Cook ▲
SOUTHERN ALPS
Christchurch
Canterbury Plains
Akaroa
Ashburton
Lake Wanaka
Mt Aspiring ▲
Timaru
Milford Sound
Lake Wakatipu
Oamaru
Queenstown
Lake Te Anau
Middlemarch
33
Te Anau
34
Dunedin

Invercargill
Bluff
Foveaux Strait
Half Moon Bay
SOUTHERN OCEAN
Stewart Island

28 Bay of Islands Vintage Railway
29 The *Northern Explorer*
30 Wellington to Wairarapa
31 Glenbrook Vintage Railway
32 The *TranzAlpine*
33 *The Seasider*
34 Taieri Gorge Railway

- - - - State boundaries
———— Train lines
◯ Cities and prominent towns

0   100   200 miles

0   100   200 km